BASQUE SOCIETY

The Center for Basque Studies at the University of Nevada, Reno, commissioned Alfonso Pérez-Agote, president of the Centro de Estudios sobre la Identidad Colectiva (CEIC, the Center for Studies on Collective Identity) to undertake this work. It follows the general guidelines established by the CEIC project, and most of its research team has contributed to it. However, for some chapters (3, 6, and 11) the CEIC has benefited from the participation of outside scholars. The book's editors also are CEIC members.

The Center for Studies on Collective Identity (http://www.ehu.es/CEIC) is a group dedicated to research, reflection, and debate on questions related to identity in contemporary society. It is made up of professors and researchers mostly linked to the Department of Sociology 2 at the Universidad del País Vasco / Euskal Herriko Unibertsitatea (UPV/EHU, University of the Basque Country). It holds important posts such as the presidency of the Comité de Recherche Identité, Espace, et Politique (CRI, the Research Committee on Identity, Space, and Politics) in the Association Internationale des Sociologues en Langue Française (AISLF, the International Association of Sociologists in the French Language) and the secretariat of the Research Committee on Social Movements, Collective Action and Social Change (RC48) in the International Sociological Association (ISA).

Basque Society

Structures, Institutions, and Contemporary Life

Basque Textbooks Series

Centro de Estudios sobre la Identidad Colectiva
Edited by Gabriel Gatti, Ignacio Irazuzta, and Iñaki Martínez de Albeniz

Translated by Cameron J. Watson

Center for Basque Studies
University of Nevada, Reno

This book was published with generous financial support from the Basque Government.

Library of Congress Cataloging-in-Publication Data

Basque society : structures, institutions, and contemporary life / edited by Gabriel Gatti, Ignacio Irazuzta, and Iñaki Martínez de Albeniz.
p. cm. -- (Basque textbooks series)
ISBN 978-1-877802-25-6 Paperback
ISBN 978-1-877802-27-0 Hardcover
ISBN 978-1-877802-27-1 Compact disk
1. País Vasco (Spain)--Social conditions. 2. País Vasco (Spain)--Economic conditions.
3. País Vasco (Spain)--Politics and government. 4. País Vasco (Spain)--Social life and customs. 5. País Vasco (Spain) I. Gatti, Gabriel. II. Irazuzta, Ignacio. III. Martínez de Albeniz, Iñaki. IV. Series.
HN590.P28G38 2005
946'.608--dc22

2005031098

Published by the Center for Basque Studies
University of Nevada, Reno /322
Reno, Nevada 89557-0012

Printed in the United States of America

CONTENTS

Gabriel Gatti, Ignacio Irazuzta, Iñaki Martínez de Albeniz

Introduction

WHAT IS the Basque Country? Or rather, what are we referring to when we talk about the Basque Country? The Basque Country is a complex reality. In principle, such a statement might seem trite—all social reality is, after all, complex—if we didn't add why this particular case is so complex. The complexity of the Basque case stems from a basic lack of overlap in its cultural, economic, political, and social frontiers. However, this phenomenon—the multiplicity and lack of concurrence between these frontiers—has, through its very ubiquity, become increasingly socially obvious and even sociologically trivial in modern global societies. It would be difficult, then, to classify the Basque Country as an exclusive case. Beyond such generalities, the principal interest in the Basque case results from the fact that this lack of concurrence in its economic, social, political, and cultural features is the product not so much of a relatively recent process (like that of globalization, for example), but rather of a convulsed history. This is what has made Basque society and the sociological issues that underpin this work complex and stimulating objects of study.

As a demonstration of the complexity that characterizes the reality described in the following pages, there is not even one single term to refer to the object under study here. (See the Glossary, for example, for an explanation of various words.) Several different terms are commonly used: "País Vasco" (from Spanish, literally meaning the "Basque Country"), "Euskadi" (from Basque, a term originally used to denote the Basque Country, but that has more recently come to refer to the Basque Autonomous Community), "Comunidad Autónoma Vasca" (from Spanish, literally meaning the

Nature as culture
The Aitzkorri mountain range, Gipuzkoa. The mountainous terrain is one of the natural images used to characterize the identity of the inhabitants of the Basque Country. In the words of Miguel de Unamuno, "in the Basque landscape, everything appears to be within one's reach and made in proportion to the people who live there and give it life; it is a domestic, familial landscape where one sees more land than sky; it is a nest."
Photo: Iñaki Martínez de Albeniz.

"Basque Autonomous Community"), and "Euskal Herria" (from Basque, literally meaning "the land of Basque speakers," but that has also come to mean the entire Basque Country). These terms refer to several of the various dimensions that make up Basque reality. Some are cultural in meaning, while others are political, administrative, or economic.

One must, however, delineate or choose one of these dimensions of Basque social reality as a starting point (and a reference point for looking at both the past and the future) in the sociological journey on which we are departing here. We will use the term "Basque Country" to denote the politico-administrative unit that was created by the passage of the Statute of Gernika in 1979, a unit that is composed of the historic territories of Araba, Gipuzkoa, and Bizkaia. In other words, our story takes place within the framework of what has come to be known via the process of political institutionalization in the Basque Country. The basic demarcation line is the recent legal-administrative crystallization of a series of the political, economic, social, and cultural processes that we will try to address in as wide a reach as possible. This is also the reason why we have chosen the term "Basque Country" (deriving from the official name stated in the Statute of Gernika, the Autonomous Community of the Basque Country) throughout this work.

HAVING THUS established this demarcation line, one must also obviously recognize that any sociology of the Basque Country will also be necessarily related to this institutionalization process. By this, we mean that it would be strange to ignore the fact that recent Basque sociology—and the present volume is but one part of this greater whole—has also contributed to the plausibility of this social reality that we term "the Basque Country." As regards the current work, such plausibility will be constructed according to three basic sociological guidelines, around which the book's three sections will be presented. Below we offer a brief sketch of these three guidelines and their respective expressions before later examining in more detail the chapters that make up each section in the present work.

The first guideline addresses sociostructural aspects of the Basque Country. Here we point out the objective face of Basque society. Through specific historical and statistical data, the student will be introduced to the main classificatory points of analysis regarding the aforementioned reality: demography, together with the territorial and socioeconomic structure. One should not, however, take "objective" to mean a mere description of certain key indicators. Rather, it is more a question of a simultaneous perspective on the social structure of the Basque Country during the previous three decades (those that coincide with what we have termed the institutionalization process), together with a longer diachronic-historical perspective demonstrating the emergence of what may be termed "the social question" in the Basque Country, the materialization of a society there in the modern sense of the word. The historical references for each of the chapters will be centered, then, on a period characterized by the transformation from tradition to modernity, a period that ultimately saw the birth of an industrial society and the emergence of the social question in the Basque Country.

ONCE THE objective bases of society have been established, the second section of the book will address the subjectivization process of this order, its interiorization (in terms of meaning) among the social actors themselves. This implies exploring one of the basic theoretical dimensions of sociology: the socialization process, or the process by which an objective order is established in a meaningful world for those who inhabit it. In this section, we will address two thematic issues as a means of addressing the processes of socialization and social reproduction in the Basque Country: socialization patterns or the agencies of socialization that contribute to the reproduction of the social order and the symbolic centers that make up this order. Here, both religion and politics will be especially relevant. In fact, one could argue that the process of modernization in the Basque Country can be explained in great part as one of transferring centrality—some authors speak of sacredness, of "consecration"—from religion to politics.

THE THIRD section of the book will concentrate more specifically on contemporary social processes in two ways. First, it will address the crisis of social institutions—principally politics, religion, and work—that from a macro point of view constitute the meaning of life and social identity. Such a crisis results in the emergence of polycentric societies in which lifeworlds, out of which the social meaning of existence is formed, are multiplied. Second, this section will also address the new subjectivities (identities) that are forming in these decentered (or functionally differentiated) societies. It will also explore those areas of emerging social meaning where strong political identities are being fragmented and redefined in a terrain "beyond politics," pointing to new identities based on gender, changing work habits, Euskara (the Basque language), age, new territorialities, and so on.

SOCIOSTRUCTURAL ASPECTS

As we mentioned earlier, the initial section of the work addresses structural aspects of Basque society. We will explore its economic structure, territorial dimension, migratory movements, demographic configuration, linguistic differences, and urban composition. As the reader will see, our intention is to introduce the Basque Country through a description of what one might term its least debatable or most objective features, that is, to sketch the Basque Country as a certain reality recognizably distinct from other places. It can be done, although it is difficult for a sociologist to believe completely that reality is one distinct or objective *thing*. All social reality is the product of a long process of historical construction, and the fact that for us something might clearly seem to be an object does not necessarily mean that this reality is objectively different. Rather, throughout history it *has been constructed as objectively different*. In other words, the social sciences, and above all the social actors or people who live this reality as their own, consider it to be something singular, distinguishable, and special.

In the case of the Basque Country, the elements with which this difference is constructed stem from four distinct sources: socioeconomic (Chapter 1), sociojuridical (Chapter 2), demographic (Chapter 3) and linguistic (Chapter 4).The objectivity that today is implied by the reference "the Basque Country" has been shaped from these four bases throughout recent history.

CHAPTER 1 offers a general survey of the fault lines that opened up as a result of the processes of industrialization and modernization in the Basque Country. Here our intention is to equip the reader with guides to understanding the special position of the Basque Country within both the Spanish state and Europe. With this in mind, the chapter analyzes the territorial structure of the Basque Country and the differences that, in the realms of work, urban life, and class organization, exist between its constituent provinces, together with the consequences of this for its contemporary economic and territorial structure.

Together with its socioeconomic structure, another of the basic pillars of Basque distinctiveness is to be found in the legal, administrative, and institutional realms analyzed in Chapter 2. Here the analysis explains how what might be termed the "Basque differential factor" is represented and how, as a consequence, the

Changing institutions
The University of Oñati (Gipuzkoa) was founded in 1548 and functioned until 1902.
Photo: Iñaki Martínez de Albeniz.

---

legal argument supports a justification of the historical and cultural distinctiveness of Basqueness. Moreover, bear in mind that for sociology to analyze the legal and institutional structure of a place implies more than just describing its legal articles. It also includes confronting a cartography of its social reality in such a way as to expose how the representation of collective life is revealed through its laws and institutions.

CHAPTER 3 analyzes the principal demographic questions: demographic growth, population structure by age, the birth rate, the death rate; the ageing process, the formation of couples, fecundity, and so on. Furthermore, here we will also explore the basic features of migratory movements in the Basque Country. This data is interesting for understanding not only the composition of the Basque population, but also the shape of its most characteristic social, imaginary, symbolic, political, and ideological networks. Moreover, such analysis allows one an insight into the limits that demography and sociology use as reference points for research. That is, one can see how social science both confirms and promotes specific ways of imagining the limits of social reality and how it contributes (through such analysis) to converting the places it analyzes into existent realities.

EUSKARA, or the Basque language—its existence, use, and the social values associated with it—is one of the most singular and special cultural possessions in the Basque Country. In other chapters, we analyze aspects of the language more directly related to the social construction of identity or, more specifically, to the symbolic aspects of the language: how the language serves to mark out differences and how Euskara has been constructed—beyond whether one speaks it or not—as a symbol of identity. In Chapter 4, some of the basic data surrounding the objective situation of this language will be presented: the distribution of knowledge of Euskara by age, region, and historic territory, together with several features associated with its contemporary use and promotion. The goal here is to understand the importance that the language has and has had in order to construct a representation of identity-based differences in the Basque Country.

SOCIAL MECHANISMS AND INSTITUTIONS

From the local perspective of social research, the family and peer groups have been favorite sites of inquiry for social scientists interested in discovering the sociological distinctiveness of a region and in locating key ideas that help to explain the phenomenon of collective identity and nationalism. They reflect an intimate realm that is especially pertinent in understanding the subjective dimension of social belonging and its political expression. This is especially the case in the Basque Country and particularly in Basque society during and after the regime of Francisco Franco (1939–75). We explore this basic and primary form of social genesis in the next two chapters. In Chapter 5, we examine family life from the perspective of nationalist discourse. Thereafter, we consider the special role of family-based political socialization in the Basque Country during the Franco era. In this intimate realm, a kind of affective rationality operates and therefore it is especially fitting for the reproduction of the "essential" elements of nationalism, such as the national language (Euskara), whose use at the time was banned in public spaces.

A SIMILAR STRUCTURE of intersubjective life appears in Chapter 6, where we analyze the associative world of *cuadrillas* (large groups of friends) and gastronomic societies. Starting with a description of everyday life in these small groups, this chapter goes on to explore the progressively increasing density of intersubjective and associative relations in the Basque Country. This was a world that, significantly, had little to do with the high level of industrial development and urbanization that took place in the 1960s. It was then that everyday ritual practices (above all *poteo*, or going from bar to bar in groups) began to thrive, together with the flourishing of youth, gastronomic, cultural, hiking, and dance associations.

In Chapter 7 we explore the education system as one of the fundamental agencies of socialization in modern society. This is a favorite topic for sociology, given that

Urban transformation
Public housing projects in the Miribilla neighborhood, Bilbao, Bizkaia. These buildings form part of an urban renewal project in one of the city's old mining districts. *Photo: Iñaki Martínez de Albeniz.*

here we find one of the essential mechanisms used to reproduce culture in the era of the nation-state. Furthermore, it is the institutional form of this socialization agency that molds it into an object—an especially telling object for pointing out future societal forms. In the Basque case, studies of education abound, because here one can find the most important productive and reproductive mechanisms of collective identity.

IN CHAPTER 8, we explore the media to highlight the growing importance of such formal socialization agencies. At the same time as those more informal, intimate, and affective ways of reproducing the social bond (such as the family and peer groups) are diminishing, we are seeing an expanding, universalizing tendency in socialization forms. This shift has been especially rapid in the Basque Country and came about with the process of political institutionalization after the end of the Franco regime. Then, unregulated and clandestine forms of communication that formerly nourished the nationalist consciousness became public. In particular, the media made political debate public and began to establish a "sociological normalization" that privatized certain aspects of life while making others public.

IMPLICITLY, the series of chapters addressing the socialization question discuss the specific nature of the transition to modernity in the Basque Country. However, they do not explore that important area where one finds the shaping forces of society, in other words, those institutions (such as religion) that enable the construction, transmission, and reproduction of identity. Therefore Chapter 9, on religion and collective identity, focuses on an analysis of the Catholic Church and the maintenance of Euskara as an "essential" element of Basque identity. The Franco regime tried to establish complete control over the means of ideological and cultural reproduction, instituting a rigorous system of controlling public spaces through its political apparatus of administration, censure, and repression. As a result, the reproduction of any kind of ideology or culture that contravened the official regime retreated into the private sphere and to the least visible side of certain institutions that were allowed to retain a public face. This was the case with the church, which, through its organizational network, sheltered numerous activities of political socialization against the Franco regime.

It was the prominence of the political, then, that imbued the language with relevance in defining collective identity. Chapter 10, dedicated to language and collective identity, reviews the recent history of Euskara. Here we see the transformation of a Basque identity defined in ethnic or even biological terms into an identity based on sociocultural elements. This chapter recalls the historical tensions that resulted in both the decline and then the recuperation of Euskara, focusing principally on the progressive transformation of the language into a political symbol. This has implied, in turn, a complete ideological reformulation of Basque nationalism in which the language became the essential defining marker of identity.

HOWEVER, the most obvious sign of the modernization and institutionalization of political life in the Basque Country is the emergence of political parties, which we examine in Chapter 11. From the perspective of political science, we explore the translation of the social into the political that the professionalization of political life implied and its manifestation in political parties that were now able to operate publicly. The particular historical inheritance explored in the sociology of the preceding chapters has manifested itself in a party system that demonstrates the singularities of a modern class society and, even more significantly, the enclaves of a social space that different Basque nationalist political parties shared. It is within this context of institutional normalization that political science constructs its object, and it does so by analyzing the movements of political parties through the objectivity of electoral indicators. This contrasts with the predominantly subjective perspective apparent in moments of political occlusion that have been explored in previous texts and that imbue political analysis with a different temporal dimension from that of sociology.

WE ANALYZE the subjective dimension of politics once again when, in Chapter 12, we examine civil society and its social movements. The effect of nationalism in the Basque Country, with its profound network of politics, meaning, and intersubjective relations stands out in the analysis of these emerging phenomena. This theoretical approach to the subject of social movements highlights their intermediary position between politics and the social, cultural, and institutional sphere, which at least until now has made the Basque Country an especially fertile ground for its dissemination. This has been especially (although not solely) the case in the realm of radical Basque nationalism, which has traditionally cultivated emerging political spaces and converted certain social or cultural statements into political ones.

CONTEMPORARY PROCESSES: IDENTITY, CULTURE, AND EVERYDAY LIFE

At the beginning of this introduction, we argued that the appearance of political institutionalization heralded a decisive change for the Basque Country. This is because it marked the transformation a society in which where politics protected social reality like a kind of sacred canopy, endowing it with meaning, into another in which politics was decentralized and went on to expand meaning in a random sense under the same conditions as other spheres of reality. In the third section of the book, we take a look at the spheres of social meaning that encouraged these new subjectivities, the most significant of which were new unconventional forms of politics based on Euskara, the new work cultures, gender, younger generations, and new territorial realities.

The goal of Chapter 13 is to evaluate the effects that this process of change had on the way in which people have conceived and experienced politics. The conclusion drawn by Basque political sociology is not, however, unanimous: Some observers argue that this political institutionalization implied a depoliticization of society, while others point out the opposite, namely, that it gave rise to a "politicization" of social spheres—the private realm, work, culture, and so on—that were previously not considered political or susceptible to politicization, in short, that political institutionalization was accompanied by a repoliticization of society.

The Basque language, Euskara, forms another of the social and sociological realms that underwent a profound transformation following the process of political institutionalization, and Chapter 14 deals with this change. In other chapters we analyze the importance of Euskara in constructing national identity in the Basque Country. Here our challenge is to demonstrate the role and place that the language has occupied during the era of political institutionalization. During this period, definitions of Basque identity became more flexible and the borders between different communities became more open in such a way that subjects previously excluded from the possibility of calling themselves "Basque" (for ethnocultural, political, linguistic, or social reasons) could now assume a Basque identity.

ANOTHER OF THE elements that acquire special relevance in societies that are more and more differentiated is the generational factor, as analyzed in Chapter 15, which explores the connections between generational and social change in the Basque Country. Here, we address youth as a social, rather than essentialist, construction, open to being articulated in different ways with other social categories. We also give special

Cultural symbols
Boinas Elosegui, a store specializing in Basque headwear. Evidence confirms that the Basque beret or txapela was already in common use in the seventeenth century, originally in Gipuzkoa and Navarre. It has subsequently become one of the most distinctive pieces of Basque clothing, and has even been incorporated into the uniform of the Basque autonomous police force.
Photo: Iñaki Martínez de Albeniz.

---

attention to the changing relations between youth, identity, and politics through a comparative analysis of two distinct phases of recent Basque history in which young people—although in different ways, both from the point of view of social articulation and that of sociological analysis—played a prominent role: the period of social and political agitation coinciding with the rise of ETA in the 1960s and the later emergence of the Basque punk movement in the 1980s, politically more careful and less predictable in its cultural makeup and therefore coinciding with political institutionalization.

CHAPTER 16 explores one of those areas in which the social role of young people is being redefined: the world of work, a social realm intimately involved in a process of rapid transformation as a consequence of the economic restructuring that has taken place during the last twenty-five years on both a local and a global scale. Perhaps the least examined aspect of these changes, analyzed in detail from both structural and quantitative points of view, has been the role that new representations based on work have played in constructing social identity. This chapter summarizes those sociological theories that question the traditional work model (salaried and industrial), noting its deficiency in explaining the complex reality of work in contemporary societies.

A similar case occurs with another mark around which one of the most conspicuous identities of contemporary society is constituted: those based on gender. Chapter 17 explores gender as one of the basic aspects around which new identifications are shaped, both in the Basque academic realm (the institutionalization of gender studies as a distinct discipline and its close connection, as in the rest of Western society, to political mobilization) and in the more specifically political dimension of gender, channeled through both feminism and nationalism, as well as gender-based institutional politics. Finally, this chapter examines the social and identity-based gender issues through the analysis of one ritual, highly visible as a result of media interest, that in recent years has questioned the traditional roles of men and women: the *alardes* (literally, "military parades") of Hondarribia and Irún in Gipuzkoa.

It is no longer surprising, in an increasingly globalized world, to observe that the notion of diaspora serves as one of the principal challenges to those who defend a traditional or conventional form of understanding territoriality, the ground on which identities come into play in a postmodern world where the nation-state is no longer as central and defining. Chapter 18 attempts to bring together various issues in one social phenomenon, from the most traditional notion of diaspora as a traumatic exodus of peoples to contemporary social phenomena such as immigration for economic reasons, political exile, and traditional migratory ethnic transnational workers and communities, all phenomena of which Basques are good examples. This chapter also analyzes the resources used to institutionalize the Basque diaspora, thereby confronting the identity-based challenge that this diaspora implies.

THE THIRD part of the book concludes with a general reflection on the changing dimension of collective identity in the Basque Country today. If there is one irrefutable demonstration of the processes of social change affecting Basque society, it is that, as opposed to univocal and spherical expressions of identity in previous eras, the current panorama indicates multiple and increasingly flexible identities to such an extent that one can even begin to argue that partial, spontaneous, and ephemeral identities are now dominant. In order to illustrate this general transformation of the dynamics and language of identity, in Chapter 19, we end with a brief ethnography of a Bilbao neighborhood, San Francisco, where one can observe the multiple fronts on which these new subjectivities are unfolding.

Our exploration ends with an epilogue that raises an issue that has yet to be fully accounted for; a work in progress that explains its tentative nature. We began this introduction by alluding to the importance sociology has had in the process of political institutionalization in the

Basque Country. To put it simply, Basque sociology has had a performative effect on Basque social reality, since, in part at least, it has contributed to shaping this reality as both an object of study and a context of life. However, the reverse is also true: Basque social reality and its vicissitudes, above all its general historical experience and the different generational contributions of those who have addressed Basque society, have influenced the form in which this same reality has shaped "its" sociology. As a consequence, the epilogue attempts, reflexively, to begin thinking sociologically about Basque sociology. Indeed, this mutual construction of both Basque society and its sociology is a central feature of the book, even when it is not explicitly stated as such.

Section 1: Sociostructural aspects

Idoia Martín (with Andrés G. Seguel)

1 · Structures

Socioeconomic, territorial, urban

SUMMARY

This chapter offers a general overview of the process of industrialization and modernization in the Basque Country. It seeks to provide a series of guides with which to understand the special nature of this process within both the Spanish state and Europe. The special dimension of this process is best understood in terms of the territorial structure of the Basque Country, different patterns of work, urbanization and class organization in each of the Basque provinces, and the economic and territorial structure of the Basque Country.

THE DEVELOPMENT of a worldwide capitalist market in the nineteenth century brought about a new international division of labor in which vast colonial, semicolonial, and underdeveloped regions became suppliers of primary materials for developed countries and importers of manufactured and capital goods. The industrialization and development of a capitalist mode of production in the Basque Country between 1876 and 1914 took place within this dynamic.

THE PROCESS OF MODERNIZATION AND INDUSTRIALIZATION

Industrial Europe, and particularly Great Britain, needed the phosphorous-free iron ore that was plentiful in the Bizkaia basin. The advantages offered by this area—the proximity of these deposits to a major port (Bilbao), their location in compact, surface-level, and easy to mine layers, the homogeneous nature of the iron ore and its high metallic content, together with the development of important return shipping routes—resulted in a number of Basque and foreign companies being formed, from the early 1870s onward, to mine and export this iron.

This industrialization, which first appeared in Bizkaia and Gipuzkoa during the mid-nineteenth century, did not take place evenly throughout the Basque Country. Although Bizkaia was more or less completely industrialized in the nineteenth century, Gipuzkoa had to wait until at least 1920. Araba, in turn, waited further still until reaching a comparable level with the coastal provinces. Industrialized Bizkaia was obviously an important influence on Gipuzkoan economic progress in the twentieth century, just as the two coastal provinces then played an important role in the growth of their interior counterpart during the final phase of Basque economic development. However, having said that, each province also followed its own path to industrialization with its own particular characteristics.

DESPITE the diversity of situations and circumstances, however, there were some common features within this industrialization process in the Basque Country. From the late nineteenth century onward, Bizkaian economic hegemony was more and more evident, to the extent that, in spite of the relative autonomy of the processes of industrialization in the other territories of the Basque Country, Bizkaia's importance as the leading producer would bear down on the economic structure of the Basque Country as a whole. The feature that was already apparent at the beginning of the Bizkaian industrial revolution and that would remain a constant for a long time to come was its orientation toward the iron and steel industry, which meant that iron production became the most important industry. The iron and steel sector subsequently retained a leading role when development spread to the other historic territories, which also came to depend on the production and transformation of iron

Past glories
A rusting boat on the left bank of the Bilbao estuary. Bizkaia, and especially Bilbao, underwent major industrialization. The formerly potent naval sector, however, has suffered a long process of decline.
Photo: Iñaki Martínez de Albeniz.

---

as a pillar of their economic bases, although, as we noted, in the other historic territories, the relative importance of the iron and steel sector never reached that of Bizkaia.

THE SUPREMACY of this sector also brought with it certain weaknesses that would affect the entire Basque economic structure. Because the whole economic structure depended on iron and steel, it suffered greatly when the demand for iron fell. Furthermore, the lesser importance of the remaining economic activities prevented them from sustaining and maintaining economic stability. To a certain extent, then, the dominance of the iron and steel sector ultimately represented a real economic weakness.

Also, the industrial revolution came relatively late to the Basque Country. This might not seem so obvious if we compare the Basque case with what happened in Spain, since Bizkaia and Gipuzkoa modernized their economies well before most Spanish regions. Yet it is more apparent if we situate Basque development within that of Europe as a whole. The late arrival of industrialization in the Basque Country had serious consequences. The Basque bourgeoisie had to overcome a significant disparity as regards European industrial levels that had been attained many years previously, and this implied massive investment. Such investment could be carried out only by a very small group who were financially able to fund what had to be (already at its birth) a major industry.

THE DELAY with which the Basque Country underwent industrialization had another specific consequence: the necessity of the Spanish market for the Basque economy to consume its products. Europe was not an option, since the existent technical imbalance implied high and uncompetitive costs against those in European countries, which, moreover, also imposed tariff barriers. In turn, the Basque bourgeoisie favored a protectionist policy to prevent European products from flooding into Spain.

Basque industrialization created an economy whose productive capacity surpassed the reduced level of the Basque Country itself to consume its output. At the same time, the Basque Country could not supply the workforce needed to maintain this industrial structure. It thus turned to "importing" a workforce. Bizkaia and, in successive waves, Gipuzkoa and Araba, attracted workers from other provinces in the Spanish state (see Section 1, Chapter 3), who abandoned an agricultural sector that, in general, restricted them to low socioeconomic lifestyles. Of course, not all the workforce was imported, because many Basque peasants also abandoned the land to move to urban centers and work in industry. However it is still true that, above all in the most intense stages of development, immigrants formed the majority among the industrial workforce.

THE PRODUCTIVE AND BUSINESS STRUCTURE

THE PREDOMINANCE of the Basque Country in heavy industry, capital goods, and the service sector (banks, insurance agencies, and shipping companies) is closely linked to the historical process by which the bourgeoisie was formed and capital accumulated. This process revolved around a reduced group of noteworthy businessmen (merchant bankers, whose wealth came from commercial capital acquired in the eighteenth and nineteenth centuries; mine owners involved in both mineral production and export; and a nascent industrial bourgeoisie) and involved the technical opportunities that emerged in the last third of the nineteenth century as a consequence of the Basque Country's status as an important mining area. This bourgeoisie knew how to make the most of a historical opportunity that presented itself during the last third of that century, working together and investing their wealth in the creation of new businesses and productive sectors. In the long run, the large Basque industrial and financial bourgeoisie became the leading group in the Spanish ruling class, increasing their participation in the Spanish economy thanks to the policy of increasing protectionism.

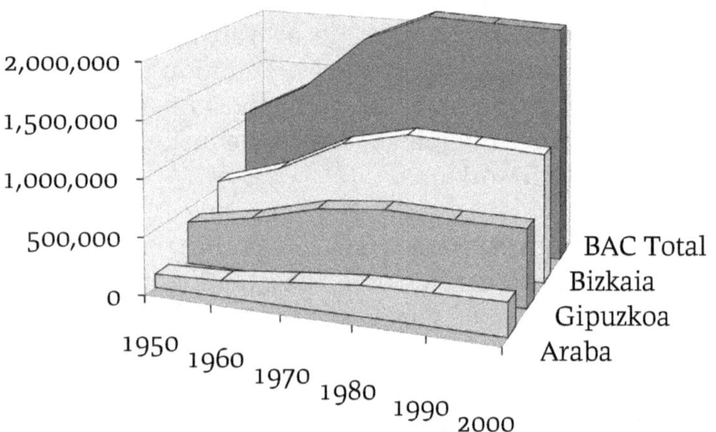

Table 1

	Araba	Gipuzkoa	Bizkaia	BAC Total
1950	118,012	374,040	569,188	1,061,240
1960	138,934	478,337	754,383	1,371,654
1970	204,323	631,003	1,043,310	1,878,636
1981	260,580	692,986	1,181,401	2,134,967
1991	276,457	676,307	1,156,245	2,109,009
2001	286,387	673,563	1,122,637	2,082,587

Population of the Basque Autonomous Community
In the second half of the twentieth century, the population of the Basque Autonomous Community nearly doubled, largely as a result of the immigration of people attracted by significant industrial development in the region between the 1950s and the 1970s.
Source: EUSTAT (The Basque Institute of Statistics), 2000.

The estuary and mining basin in and around Greater Bilbao was also one of the determining factors in the economic development and iron-and-steel-based industrial typology of the Basque Country and in the business structure that developed in Bizkaia and Gipuzkoa. In Bizkaia, the estuary traversing Greater Bilbao formed the geographical hub of its industrial and demographic revolution and was the focal point where almost all the large Basque companies and banks were located. In Gipuzkoa, on the other hand, where industrialization was much slower, it was more dispersed among several towns in small and medium-sized companies. As regards Araba, its economy scarcely changed very much at the beginning of this industrialization process, remaining primarily agricultural. It was only during the second great wave of industrialization (1953–75) that this province witnessed a significant change in its economic activity toward the industrial and service sectors.

THE TERRITORIAL AND URBAN STRUCTURE

Generally speaking, one might say that the territorial structure of the Basque Autonomous Community (BAC) is marked by a high urban density (83 percent of the population live in towns of more than ten thousand inhabitants, and 43 percent in the principal cities of each province—Bilbao in Bizkaia, Vitoria in Araba, and San Sebastián in Gipuzkoa). However, there is also a noteworthy and at times surprising coexistence between some highly industrialized areas and others where lifestyles, cultural worlds, political networks, and so on more closely resemble those of the rural world.

THESE ARE statistics demonstrating that the particular process of modernization in the Basque Country shaped its territorial structure. Effectively, as one can see in Table 1, the 1950s and 1960s marked a milestone

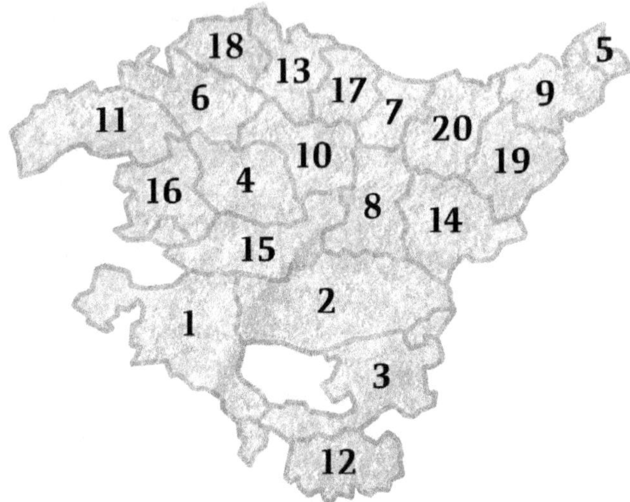

Regions of the Basque Autonomous Community

1. *Arabako Ibarrak / Valles Alaveses*
2. *Arabako Lautada / Llanada Alavesa*
3. *Arabako Mendialdea / Montaña Alavesa*
4. *Arrati-Nerbio / Arratia-Nervión*
5. *Bidasoa Beherea / Bajo Bidasoa*
6. *Bilbo Handia / Gran Bilbao (Greater Bilbao)*
7. *Deba Beherea / Bajo Deba (Low Deba)*
8. *Deba Garaia / Alto Deba (High Deba)*
9. *Donostialdea / Donostia-San Sebastián*
10. *Durangaldea / Duranguesado*
11. *Enkartazioak / Encartaciones*
12. *Errioxa Arabarra / Rioja Alavesa*
13. *Gernika-Bermeo*
14. *Goierri*
15. *Gorbeia Inguruak / Estribaciones del Gorbea*
16. *Kantauri Arabarra / Cantábrica Alavesa*
17. *Markina-Ondarroa / Marquina-Ondarroa*
18. *Plentzia-Mungia / Plencia-Munguía*
19. *Tolosaldea / Tolosa*
20. *Urola Kostaldea / Urola Costa*

defined by the strong increase in the immigrant population that we have already noted. In the main, these people were attracted by the industrial development of some areas in two of the historic territories: Gipuzkoa and, principally, Bizkaia, which grew by 59.2 and 53.2 percent respectively between 1950 and 1970. In the case of Araba, its fundamentally rural-based population maintained a certain stability through to the 1980s. Then, as a result of the concentration of administrative services in its capital, Vitoria (the seat of the new Basque Autonomous Government), the population grew by 77 percent in the period 1970 to 1980, with all the consequences that this implied for the urban structure of the province.

Thus, if we look at each of the three territories that currently make up the Basque Autonomous Community we can identify three different kinds of territorial and urban structure. Araba's most pronounced feature is the concentration of people in its capital, Vitoria during the 1980s, when the administrative capital of the BAC was located there. It subsequently became home to three-quarters of the territory's population. Therefore, what we might term the "Araba structure" was established around the hegemony of the capital city, which came to define demographic growth and economic activity in the rest of the (predominantly rural) territory.

BIZKAIA, on the other hand, was already characterized at the end of the nineteenth century by a concentration of people in its capital, Bilbao, and along the banks of the Nervión River, which runs through the city. This area was characterized, until quite recently and through both its architecture and the steps followed in its general urbanization process, by the strong industrial nature of economic activity in Bizkaia. The region formed by Greater Bilbao contained at one point as much as 80 percent of Bizkaia's population and 44 percent of the BAC's, while more rural regions of Bizkaia, such as Arratia-Nervión and Encartaciones, experienced lower demographic growth. In turn, in recent years, Bizkaia's intermediate regions have experienced the most growth—the Duranguesado, in the interior, as an extension of Bilbao's economic activity, and the region between Plencia and Munguía as a residential area.

GIPUZKOA stands out for the even growth and stable development of its capital city, San Sebastián, together with several regional urban centers, such as Irún, Errenteria, Eibar, Bergara, and Mondragón. Consequently, of the three historic territories, it has the most even sociospatial structure and lacks a hegemonic urban dynamic. Its territorial structure is characterized by one feature: multiple centrality.

THE WORK AND CLASS STRUCTURE

Industrialization has been, without any doubt, the most important phenomenon in the contemporary history of the Basque Country. Indeed, its influence exceeds that of the purely economic sphere to embrace all areas of Basque life. It is impossible to understand later demographic and social transformations without taking account of how this revolutionary economic reconstruction took place. Nor can one comprehend the particular nature of Basque political dynamics since the late nineteenth century without first considering the form in which the industrial revolution influenced both the behavior and the thought patterns of those who inhabited the Basque Country.

As nascent Basque industrialization gradually centered in Bizkaia and Gipuzkoa, a new modern demographic era began. This was characterized by the rhythm of its growth and by the location of its population (in industrial urban sprawls), as well as by changes in

Modern industry
The Acería Compacta de Bizkaia (ACB, Compact Steelworks of Bizkaia). After the economic recession of 1975–85, Basque industry was forced to become more streamlined and subsequently managed to achieve high production levels once again.
Photo: Iñaki Martínez de Albeniz.

demographic rates (birth, death, and marriage—see Section 1, Chapter 3). In Bizkaia, where industrialization developed around the Bilbao estuary, the area accounted for 84.5 percent of demographic growth in the historic territory between 1857 and 1900, mainly as a result of immigration. By contrast, in Gipuzkoa, growth was more moderate and increased only after 1900.

These differences were also evident in the makeup of the working class in the two historic territories, as regards their organizational level (greater in Bizkaia than in Gipuzkoa), social activity, and politico-ideological development, with the overwhelming dominance of socialism in Bizkaia over any other ideology associated with the working-class movement.

Its ethnocultural composition also varied greatly. For example, in the industrial towns of Gipuzkoa, the working class was basically native to the territory, still connected to the rural communities, and affected by the recent sudden changes in the Basque Country, such as the two nineteenth-century civil conflicts (the Carlist Wars) and the removal of the *fueros* (traditional laws, norms, and customs guaranteeing Basque rights). These events are extremely important for explaining certain cultural, religious, ideological, and political differences within the Basque working class. In the area around the Bilbao estuary, on the other hand, as we have seen, strong demographic growth was based principally on the immigration of people from outside the Basque Country and from a different cultural background from that of the locals. This variable was thus especially important in both the ideological construction and social composition of Basque nationalism.

IN BIZKAIA, social unrest between the classes that first experienced industrialization, the mine-owning and factory-owning bourgeoisie and the proletariat, was initially direct, confrontational, and often violent. In these conflicts, the leading protagonists were the miners, who used violence as their best tactic, not so much in search of political or revolutionary goals, but rather to achieve labor-related objectives: In other words, this was negotiation through revolt.

THE CURRENT ECONOMIC SITUATION

Basque economic development has been conditioned by that of the Spanish economy, with both sharing common features. However, the Basque economy also displays distinct and specific features. For example, for many decades, its growth was based on the specialization of a few sectors, while the Spanish economy displayed a more diversified structure. This strong specialization in the Basque economy has served to make its cyclical behavior more pronounced in both periods of expansion and periods of decline.

Before the 1975 crisis, the Basque Country enjoyed slightly higher growth rates than the Spanish average as a result of its specialization in the most dynamic sectors of this period of economic development—in the industrial sector in general and, more specifically, in metal conversions.

Between 1975 and 1985, the Basque economy underwent a period of stagnation, characterized by a fall in both demand and employment. During this period, the accumulative annual growth rate of its GNP (gross national product) was slightly negative at the same time as the number of workers in the Basque Country fell by one hundred and fifty thousand, one hundred thousand of whom came from the industrial sector.

IN THE PERIOD from 1985 to 1991, the Basque economy entered an expansionist phase. The GNP grew at a faster rate than that of the Spain as a whole, especially in 1988 and 1989, with very high figures of 6.7 percent and 6.1 percent respectively. The engine of this economic turnaround was the industrial sector, whose favorable trend was the result of an intense process of productive and work-related redeployment centered on technological modernization and of a productive reorientation through investment in rationalization and personnel readjustment with the goal of raising productivity and adapting to growing international competition. This streamlining process centered mainly on large companies, especially those involved in the iron and steel sector, domestic appliances, and electronic components. These were, in fact, the sectors on which Basque economic activity had been principally based. However, in practice, this rationalization of labor and production affected all companies located in the Basque Country.

In 1992 and especially in 1993, there was a strong recession in the Basque economy, following the same tendency in both the Spanish and international economies. In 1992, the GNP grew only minimally by 1 percent, falling to minus 0.7 percent in 1993. Industrial production followed the same evolution, with obviously negative consequences for the employment rate. The service sector, on the other hand, demonstrated positive growth rates and during these two years managed to sustain Basque economic activity.

IN 1994, ANOTHER change took place, leading to a tendency that has been maintained to this day. Of special relevance was the development of the Basque economy in 1998: a high GNP growth rate (5.2 percent) and large-scale job creation. One of the key factors in these positive economic results was the healthy state of the industrial sector. This renewed dynamism of Basque industry was in large part due to modernization and the expansion of Basque companies abroad thanks to strong ties to the expanding European industrial sector. One only has to take account of the fact that 42 percent of industrial production at this time was being exported, with 66 percent of this destined for the European market.

The construction sector also demonstrated an important increase in its activity (5.9 percent), clearly benefiting from the reduction of mortgage rates. As regards the service sector, it grew at a rate of 3.8 percent, resulting in an estimated 5 percent increase in employment. The most dynamic subsectors were company-related service industries and those related to consumption, especially commerce and above all tourist services, encouraged in recent years by the appeal of many new tourism-related offers in the Basque Country.

As THESE fluctuations show, unemployment is a deeply rooted problem in the Basque Country. It emerged three decades ago and has still not been resolved. During the economic decline between 1975 and 1985, the unemployment rate rose from 5 percent to 24 percent. Since then, economic growth has not been able to reduce this level to less than 8.3 percent. The repercussions of this problem continue, especially for the making of collective identity in contemporary Basque society, which will be analyzed in Section 3, Chapter 16.

Several factors help to explain the origins of unemployment in the Basque Country. In the first place, the oil crisis of the mid-1970s resulted in a sharp decline in the productive sector and, as a consequence, in a reduction in employment opportunities. This crisis especially affected the Basque Country because of the strong specialization within its economy: the iron and steel industry, shipbuilding, domestic appliance white goods, and so on. These specialized sectors relied on energy consumption and older technology and were in decline all over the world.

At the same time the Basque economy suffered the consequences of not beginning a process of reconstruction toward the service sector. This would have been the natural outcome of its economic development through up to the 1970s and one that other areas with a similar industrialization process had undertaken. Ultimately,

Symbols of success
Neguri, a neighborhood of Getxo, Bizkaia. Located at the mouth of the Bilbao estuary, on its right bank, the Neguri neighborhood became the preferred residence of the city's industrial and financial bourgeoisie.
Photo: Iñaki Martínez de Albeniz.

---

then, the failure to begin such a reconstruction process prevented the Basque economy from using the service sector as a stabilizing factor during the crisis.

ELSEWHERE, in contrast to the rest of the industrial countries, problems derived from the Spanish political transition (after the death of Franco in 1975) meant that the Basque Country had to undertake measures in order to adapt to this new political context, and this also contributed to aggravating the unemployment problem. Thus, while other advanced countries attempted to prevent rising prices from leading to higher wages, in Spain, the lack of an adequate response to this problem meant that labor costs continued to rise. As a result, Spanish companies, in an attempt to regain some competitiveness, replaced labor with capital, resulting in massive layoffs. Therefore, between 1975 and 1985 the rate at which jobs were eliminated in Spain was double the European average.

Another factor that contributed to rising unemployment was an increase in the population actively seeking work. The social modernization of the country had resulted in the incorporation of women into the workplace. This led to an increase in the active work rate among the female population, although it was still far behind the European average. To this one should add that from the 1980s onward, those born in the 1960s (a significant number, because there had been a notable surge in birth rates during that decade) began to enter the workplace. As a consequence, the number of those actively seeking work in Spain grew faster than in other comparable countries.

THUS, THE origin of unemployment in the Basque Country is the result of an immediate factor (the oil crisis), a structural factor (productive specialization in older sectors with a tendency to replace workers with capital improvements, and the relatively scarce presence of the service sector), and a sociodemographic factor (the growth of the population actively seeking work).

From 1985 onward, the Basque and Spanish economies began to recover, growing at rates faster than the European average and leading to the net creation of work, although given the massive decline in job opportunities in the previous years, it was still impossible to recover this lost employment. At the same time, a structural change took place with the progressive increase in service-related activities, even if the relative importance of industry—a sector that is very susceptible to variations in the international situation—remained strong in the Basque economy.

However, the growth of the economy and of employment in the second half of the 1980s was hit suddenly by an economic crisis in the early 1990s. This actually led to record unemployment rates in the Basque Country of about 25 percent in 1994 and 1995. That said, the situation has improved considerably since then. The Basque economy has grown again, which has led to the creation of jobs and a reduction in the unemployment rate to 8.3 percent in 2002, even if it is still difficult for some groups (such as young people and women) to enter the workplace.

Lesson one

LEARNING OBJECTIVES

1. To understand the industrialization process that began in the nineteenth century and how it influenced whole areas of life—economic, social, political, and cultural.
2. To examine in depth the common features of industrialization in the Basque Country and to see how these have conditioned some of the weaknesses and strengths of the current modern economic structure.
3. To link the process followed in the formation of the bourgeoisie and the accumulation of capital to the productive structure and dominance of certain sectors in the Basque Country (heavy industry and capital goods and services such as banks, insurance agencies, and shipping companies).
4. To trace the later evolution of the Basque economy from the economic crisis in 1975 to the present day,

taking account of different periods of recession (1975–85, 1992–93) and growth (1985–91, 1994–2001) and to understand how these have influenced one of the most profound and as yet unresolved problems in the Basque Country: unemployment.

REQUIRED READING

Mercedes Arbaiza, "Labor Migration during the First Phase of Basque Industrialization: The Labor Market and Family Motivations," *History of the Family* 3, no. 2 (1998): 199–219.

María Angeles Larrea and Rafael Mieza, *Introduction to the History of the Basque Country* (Bilbao: Basque American Foundation, 1986).

SUGGESTED READING

Manuel González Portilla, ed., *100 años de historia del País Vasco* (Bilbao: Universidad del País Vasco, 1986).

Consejo Económico y Social Vasco, *Memoria anual sobre la situación socioeconómica de la CAPV, 1997, 1998, 1999, 2000* (Bilbao: Consejo Económico y Social Vasco, 1998, 1999, 2000, and 2001).

WRITTEN LESSON FOR SUBMISSION

1. To what extent did industrialization define the birth of contemporary Basque society?
2. Explain briefly how the industrialization models of Bizkaia, Gipuzkoa, and Araba differed and the results of these differences for each of the historic territories.
3. Throughout the period from 1976 to 2002, there were important structural transformations (demographic, social, and economic) that influenced both the economic structure and the labor market in the Basque Country. In what ways were these changes linked to the development of the labor market there during

this period? You may use the data supplied by INE (Instituto Nacional de Estadística, the National Statistics Institute) at www.ine.es, and EUSTAT (Euskal Estatistika Erakundea / Instituto Vasco de Estadística, the Basque Statistics Office) at www.eustat.es.

Iñaki Martínez de Albeniz

2 · Institutional structure

SUMMARY

This chapter describes the particular legal, administrative, and institutional structure of the Basque Country. It highlights the importance of legal arguments and historical differences between the Basque institutions and those of the rest of the Spanish state in constructing the idea of Basque difference. Thus, it looks at some important elements within the Basque legal and institutional framework: the concierto económico (fiscal pact) and Statute of Gernika, the fueros (traditional laws, norms, and customs), the diputaciones (provincial councils), and the historic territories.

FROM A sociological point of view, any analysis of the legal and institutional structure of a given place involves more than just a mere description of its laws. Rather, it implies addressing the broader cartography of a particular social reality so that its laws and institutions actually reveal a way of representing collective life. By understanding laws and institutions in this way, one comes to understand what criteria are used in the objectification and representation of a given place and how such representations serve as a base from which social identities are then constructed and experienced.

In effect, such laws, rules, and institutions are also forms of representing the "social," which in turn transmits ways of understanding and even helps to construct reality. Such is the case in the Basque Country, where the laws that are made and the institutions that uphold them are intersected by a threefold idiosyncrasy.

First, there are multiple ways to refer to the region: the terms "País Vasco" (from Spanish, literally meaning the

---

"Basque Country"), "Euskal Herria" (from Basque, literally meaning "the land of Basque speakers," although also used to denote the Basque Country in more general terms), and "Provincias Vascongadas" (from Spanish, literally meaning the "Basque provinces," although with an archaic connotation) are all highly charged in their meanings, not only because each implies a certain and distinct reality—cultural, administrative, political, or even just linguistic—or because choosing one of the options might point to a certain ideological bias on the part of whoever uses it, but also because these terms effectively refer to different areas—for example, some of them include Navarre and/or the French Basque Country, while others don't—and to areas with different institutional and legal structures.

Second, and linked to the first, there is also an idiosyncrasy stemming from the diversity of territorial spheres within the Basque Country and the compatibility (or lack thereof) of institutional structures in these spheres. In effect, the Basque Country is a region divided between two states: In France, it lacks any special legal or institutional status, while in Spain, it is divided between two autonomous communities (the Basque Autonomous Community and the Foral Community of Navarre), both with a high degree of administrative autonomy and a solid institutional structure.

FINALLY, there is the idiosyncrasy stemming from the coexistence of this particular institutional structure with wider social realities and official frameworks in Europe, Spain, and France, a coexistence that is often conflictive.

For the reasons already outlined in the introduction to this work, here we take as a basic frame of reference the area of the Basque Autonomous Community (BAC) and

The tree of Gernika
The Assembly House of Bizkaia, Gernika. Until 1876, this was the meeting place for the so-called General Assemblies of Bizkaia. Then, after being suspended for over one hundred years, they began to meet once again in 1979. The Statute of Gernika, the legal basis of the current politico-administrative system of the Basque Autonomous Community, was drafted here.
Photo: Iñaki Martínez de Albeniz.

---

its three historic territories, Araba, Gipuzkoa, and Bizkaia.

THE "BASQUE DIFFERENTIAL"

The system of political organization in the Basque Autonomous Community presumes the existence of what has been termed the "Basque differential." It was established on three main precepts: A historical, sociopolitical reality based on the foral system (see below for a fuller description), the cultural-linguistic dimension determined by Euskara, the Basque language, and a normative complex that justifies and furnishes legitimacy to Basque specificity.

THE FIRST additional provision to the 1978 Spanish Constitution is the key document indicating the legal-normative status of the concept of the Basque differential. This status is defined in turn by three ways in which the legal and institutional structure of the Basque Autonomous Community enjoys exclusiveness: via a particular mosaic of powers that are the exclusive domain of the government of the Basque Autonomous Community—the autonomous police force, education, highways, and so on—via a special form of provincial political organization known as *foralidad* that supports, in distinct fashion, the domestic organic system of the Basque Autonomous Community, and via the *concierto económico* (fiscal pact) system as an instrument of fiscal and financial sovereignty. Thus, within the framework of the constitution, the Basque Country is differentiated from the rest of Spain by means of its historic territories, its language, its foral civil law, its own police force, and its system of fiscal agreements.

THE STATUTE OF GERNIKA (1979)

The 1979 Statute of Gernika develops this differential legally and determines the political organization and institutional structure of the Basque Autonomous Community. Its preliminary article begins: "The Basque people or Euskal Herria, as an expression of their nationality, make up the Autonomous Community within the Spanish state under the name Euskadi or Basque Country [País Vasco], in accordance with the constitution and the current statute that is their basic institutional standard."

AUTONOMOUS ADMINISTRATIVE ORGANS

Basque Parliament

Basque Government

PROVINCIAL GOVERNMENT ORGANS

General assembly of Araba	General assembly of Bizkaia	General assembly of Gipuzkoa

Provincial council of Araba	Provincial council of Bizkaia	Provincial council of Gipuzkoa

MUNICIPAL GOVERNMENT ORGANS

City Halls

Institutional structure

The multi-layered nature of institutional organization in the Basque Autonomous Community reveals a complex interplay of different (and sometimes competing) forces at the autonomous, provincial and municipal levels.

The figure above presents a general outline of Basque institutional organization at every level.

IN ACCORDANCE with the Statute of Gernika, the Basque Autonomous Community is made up of the historic territories of Araba, Gipuzkoa, and Bizkaia while at the same time leaving open the possible incorporation of Navarre if that province so decides. Within this territorial division Euskara shares official status with Spanish.

Institutional norms imply that powers in the BAC are exercised through its parliament, government, and *lehendakari* (president). The Basque Parliament, made up of an equal number of representatives from each historic territory (a total of seventy-five, elected for a period of four years), is the institution that exercises legislative power, promotes and controls government activity, and passes governmental policy. It is the highest public institution in the Basque Country and the representative organization of the state in the BAC. The members of parliament elect the *lehendakari* from this chamber, who, in turn, appoints the head minister of each governmental department, thereby forming the autonomous executive.

THE STATUTE of Gernika defines all the powers of the BAC, both those exclusive to the autonomous community and those corresponding to the fulfillment of basic state legislation. Moreover, the statute also establishes the exclusive powers of each historic territory.

THE FORAL SYSTEM

The particular legal status of the Statute of Gernika has roots in the foral system of the Basque Country and stems from the 1978 Spanish Constitution's recognition of the foral principle. In other words, the statute is effectively a regulation that updates the historic rights of the foral system based on the *fueros*, or local legal charters.

Although the *fueros* originally designated the foundational charters of cities, in the Basque case, they were less localized and more general—in terms of both public and private law—and were awarded by the historic territories themselves as a sign of their autonomy. Whatever the case, the origin of the *fueros* was generally practiced common law: It was the product of the standard practice, the norms and customs, of a community.

Spanish autonomy statutes such as the Statute of Gernika were laws that distributed and articulated powers originating in the state, thus defining the relationship between central authority and the autonomous communities. Building on this basic general concept, certain amendments regarding the regional or national status of the autonomous communities were added later. This is because the Spanish Constitution differentiated between communities in assigning their powers and institutional organization, as well as in establishing the procedures of approving and reforming their statutes.

HOWEVER, for all that such differences may be significant, none of these statutes (even those enjoying a certain national status) can change their essential classification as, at root, a concession of state. Every statute is in this sense restricted to distributing and granting, by virtue of a political decision of the constituent power (personified in the Spanish nation or people as defined in Article 1 of the Spanish Constitution) powers that belong to the state. From this perspective the Statute of Gernika, as regards the national status of the Basque Country, is part of a wider reality indicated above.

Viewed from the point of view of the foral system, with its deep historical roots, however, this statute might be interpreted not as the concession of powers that stem from the state, but rather as the updated version of a series of rights belonging to specific politico-historical bodies: the foral territories. These rights, called historic rights, form a third reality that is external and extraneous to the Spanish Constitution, because they fall outside the realm of its decision-making power. As a result, they are exempt from any concessionary authority. That is, they receive nothing from the state except basic constitutional protection.

Authority through architecture
The spectacle of power, as revealed by the Provincial Council of Bizkaia, Bilbao. According to George Balandier, "certain places express power, impose their sacred quality, better than any explanation can."
Photo: Iñaki Martínez de Albeniz.

THE FORAL statute implies a system that allows the Basque Autonomous Community to assume responsibility for foral civil legislation (Article 10.5), education (Article 16), and an autonomous police force (Article 17). It also recognizes that the politico-historical institutions of the Basque Country, that is, of the historic communities making up the BAC, possess an original power and politico-legal character. Finally, it permits the creation of a system of self-government with its own institutions and powers, as well as its own original autonomous legal system known as the *fueros*, a right specified in two laws that expound the legislative capacity that the statute recognizes in the historic territories: the LTH (Ley de Territorios Históricos, Law of Historic Territories, 1983) and the Fiscal Pact Law (1981).

TERRITORIAL ORGANIZATION: THE HISTORIC TERRITORIES

The particular institutional structure of the Basque Autonomous Community thus combines common governmental institutions, such as its parliament and government, with foral organs. As such, the Statute of Gernika and the LTH, to the extent that they regulate the relations between the common institutions of the Basque Country and their foral counterparts, create a confederal model for the BAC in which the principle of the three historic territories' political equality is balanced out with each of their own distinct personalities. Together with the Basque Autonomous Government, then, the provincial councils form the main institutions of the BAC.

EACH OF THE three historic territories has its own institutions, with a legislative assembly and a government possessing a significant number of powers. These foral institutions define their singular nature as stemming from a traditional historical legacy.

The government of each territory is known as the *diputación* (literally "deputation," but also understood as a provincial council). It is led by the general deputy, and its powers are limited to the terrain of the historic territory in question. Consequently, these provincial councils exercise a wide range of powers that extend to certain areas such as urban development, highways, and cultural questions.

WITHIN the political and administrative structure of the Basque Autonomous Community, the three historic territories have an equal standing, and their relationship with the Basque Autonomous Government (in Spanish, Gobierno Vasco; in Basque, Eusko Jaurlaritza) implies its classification as somewhere between a federal and a looser confederal institution.

THE FISCAL PACT

One significant dimension of the Statute of Gernika is that, because it cedes to the Basque Autonomous Community the right to oversee and finance itself adequately, the BAC has its own treasury to exercise and develop these powers. The tax relations between the state and the BAC, in turn, are regulated by means of the traditional foral fiscal pact.

As such, the historic territories possess both the normative capacity and the autonomy to regulate, manage, and collect their own taxes. The fiscal pact contains, beyond a series of general principles, coordinating rules, and cooperative norms, general mutually agreed rules for when to apply autonomous or state standards or norms.

Therefore it is the Foral Treasuries that collect the taxes after having agreed on taxation rates with the state. Subsequently, the High Council of Basque Finances distributes the available quantities, and the provincial councils of the three historic territories and Basque Autonomous Government then decide what the distribution should be between them.

From a fiscal point of view, and with the aim of not allowing the application of the Statute of Gernika and the Fiscal Pact Law to stem from an unequal institutional financing situation, the Basque Autonomous Community directly transfers a part of its tax revenue to the Spanish administration to defray the general costs of certain state powers, such as foreign relations, defense and the armed forces, the customs and tariff system, and general transport infrastructure. It also establishes that the Basque contribution to the Spanish state takes the form of a quota or economic contribution to pay costs of state not covered by the BAC.

THE CURRENT fiscal pact allows for a special degree of autonomy within the Basque Country. Indeed, it would not be too exaggerated to suggest that the Basque Autonomous Government possesses almost all the economic decision-making powers normally belonging to a central state, the most obvious exception being that of deciding monetary and exchange rate policy, although these powers are now, of course, controlled by European Union institutions, rather than states. The autonomy statute and fiscal pact mean that relations between the Basque Country and the state correspond, to a certain extent, more to a confederal than to a federal system.

Lesson two

LEARNING OBJECTIVES

1. To gauge the importance of the institutional and legal structure of a society.
2. To familiarize yourself with the complex politico-legal structure of the Basque Country and to understand in more detail the special institutional and legal nature of the Basque Country.
3. To assess the level of autonomy in the Basque Country in relation to the Spanish state.

---

4. To evaluate the importance of the foral system as a foundation of this special Basque legal and political system in the context of the Spanish state.

REQUIRED READING

A special edition of the online journal *Euskonews & Media* 51 (October 1999), published by Eusko Ikaskuntza (the Basque Studies Society) about the Statute of Gernika: http://suseoo.su.ehu.es/euskonews/0051zbk/portada.html.

The official Web site of the Basque Autonomous Government, to get some basic information about its institutional structure: http:// www.lehendakaritza.ejgv.euskadi.net/r48-352/es//estatu_i.htm. (Click on "en" in the upper left-hand corner for an English version.)

SUGGESTED READING

The Statute of Gernika (in English) can be accessed, together with other documents, at http://www.lehendakaritza.ejgv.euskadi.net/r48-2312/en/contenidos/informacion/estatuto_guernica/en_455/estatu_com_i.html.

WRITTEN LESSON FOR SUBMISSION

1. Critically consider how the idea of the "Basque differential" was constructed and assess how this has gradually assumed legal and institutional expression.
2. Evaluate the achievement of Basque political autonomy and compare it with other international political systems.

Marta Luxán

3 · Demographic growth and migration

SUMMARY

This chapter analyzes the principal demographic characteristics of the Basque Country: demographic measures of growth, population structure by age, marriage rates, death rates, ageing, couple formation, fecundity, and so on. It also examines the basic characteristics of the migratory movements that have characterized the recent history of the Basque Country.

WITHOUT any doubt, 1975 was a watershed in the demographic history and behavior of the Basque Country, a dividing line marked by the death of the dictator, Francisco Franco and by the first effects of an economic crisis resulting from rising oil prices. It was at this time that the Bilbao Chamber of Commerce published what is considered to be the first contemporary demographic study regarding the three historic territories that today make up the Basque Autonomous Community. This was no coincidence, since the coming economic crisis and the beginning of the democratic transition marked the start of a so-called demographic crisis and together formed the initial stimulus for the development of population studies.

Three years later, in 1978, another important event in Basque demography took place: the creation of the Basque Institute of Statistics (Instituto Vasco de Estadística, EUSTAT).[1] The object of demographic study is population. This aggregate of individuals delimits and shapes the results that one might obtain from the perspective of their essential life processes, the forms in which they define them, together with the territorial demarcations to which they refer. The creation of

EUSTAT has allowed access to previously inaccessible information about the Basque population, in terms of both its nature and its disintegration, and has established the Basque Autonomous Community as an obligatory area of reference. When the Basque Autonomous Community became a specific reference for demographic study, this helped considerably in institutionalizing its (at the time embryonic) administrative reality (See Section 1, Chapter 2).

DEMOGRAPHIC TRENDS

In broad terms, between 1975 and the present, in the Basque Country, the general tendency of migratory movements has been reversed, the age structure has been transformed, and, following an era when marriages and births were on the rise, we now find one of the lowest total crude marriage rates (CMRs) and Crude Birth Rates (CBRs) in Europe. The crude marriage rate is the ratio of the total number of marriages to the total population in a specified period, while the rude birth rate is the ratio of the live births in a specified period (usually one calendar year) to the average population in that period. Their decline has led some experts to speak of a demographic crisis in the Basque Country.

BETWEEN 1950 and 1975, the population of what is today known as the Basque Autonomous Community practically doubled, reaching more than two million inhabitants by the end of this period, with half of the growth the direct or indirect result of migration. The evolution of the Basque population at this time was linked closely to an industrialization process that transformed the Basque Autonomous Community into a migratory center of attraction. In similar fashion, the subsequent industrial crisis had a clear effect on the stagnation of the population after 1975, as well as on

The future of Basque society
Children playing in a park. Demography in the situation of everyday life, with Basque children playing in one of the many parks that accompany new construction projects.
Photo: Iñaki Martínez de Albeniz.

its decline after 1981. As a consequence, the population of the Basque Autonomous Community rose from 2,072,430 in 1975 to only 2,082, 587 in 2001.

As is well known, population growth stems from two components: net migration (immigrants minus emigrants) and natural increase (births minus deaths). In the Basque case, the population loss experienced between 1981 and 1991 can be put down to the fact that negative net migration exceeded a positive natural increase, yet after 1991, both components were negative.

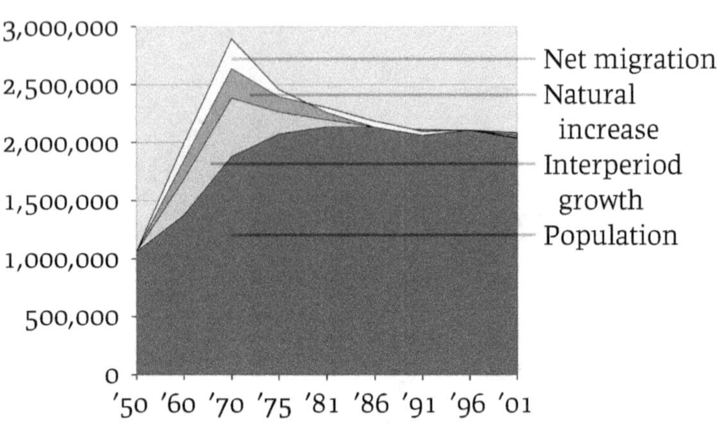

Table 2

	Population	Interperiod growth	Natural increase	Net Migration
1950	1,061,240	0	0	0
1960	1,371,654	310,414	158,188	152,226
1970	1,878,636	506,982	250,884	256,098
1975	2,072,430	193,794	128,515	65,279
1981	2,134,967	62,537	104,403	- 41,866
1986	2,133,002	- 1,965	53,394	- 55,359
1991	2,109,009	- 23,993	10,363	- 34,356
1996	2,107,307	- 1,702	- 993	- 709
2001	2,082,587	- 24,720	- 15,780	- 8,940

Population totals and growth components
After 1975, as a consequence of the economic crisis resulting from rising oil prices, job opportunities were more limited in the Basque Autonomous Community, and immigration decreased. This gradually led to greater emigration throughout the 1980s and 1990s and to a reduced overall population.
Source: EUSTAT (The Basque Institute of Statistics) and INE (The National Statistics Institute).

That is, more people died than were born, and more left than settled in the Basque Country.

POPULATION STRUCTURE BY AGE AND EVOLUTION OF THE BASIC INDICATORS

In Table 3, we can see the effect of these changes on the age structure of the Basque Country.

BETWEEN 1975 and 1981, people sixty-five years old and over doubled their overall proportion as a percentage of the population as a whole, growing from 8.25 percent to practically 17 percent. By contrast, the youngest age group (those under twenty years of age), has fallen by more than half between 1975 and 2001. The middle age group, those theoretically of a working age, increased their relative proportion within the overall

Table 3

	Population	Ages (%) 0–19	20–64	65 and over
1975	2,072,430	36.40	55.35	8.25
1981	2,134,967	34.32	56.58	9.10
1986	2,133,002	30.19	59.60	10.21
1991	2,109,009	24.09	62.46	13.45
1996	2,107,307	19.47	64.46	16.06
2001	2,082,587	18.12	64.90	16.98

Population evolution and its distribution
Between 1975 and 2001, the population in the Basque Autonomous Community became considerably more elderly, with people sixty-five and over occupying a greater proportion of the overall total at the expense of those aged nineteen and under.
Source: EUSTAT (The Basque Institute of Statistics).

Table 5

	TFR (Women)*	AMA*	TFR (Men)	APA	EMB (%)
1975	2.7	28.6	2.6	31.8	1.4
1981	1.8	28.6	1.8	31.4	3.7
1986	1.2	29.1	1.3	31.9	5.9
1991	1.0	30.0	1.0	33.0	8.0
1996	0.9	31.3	0.9	33.8	10.5
2001	1.0**	32.2**	0	0	16.3

Evolution of fertility

During the last quarter of the twentieth century, fertility rates in the Basque Autonomous Community for both women and men fell by more than 50 percent, to below the basic population replacement level. At the same time, within these general fertility rates, extramarital births increased dramatically, although within two-parent de facto relationships.

*Source: EUSTAT (The Basque Institute of Statistics) * in 1975–76, 1980–81, 1985–86, 1990–91, and 1995–96 and INE (The National Statistics Institute) ** in 2000.*

population, but only moderately. From this, we might deduce that, during the last quarter of the twentieth century, the Basque population has aged significantly and that this process has been accelerated by the progressive decline of the crude birth rate. This ageing process has been accompanied by a rising life expectancy and marked by noteworthy gender differences: There are more and more people over sixty-five years of age, and within this age group, the relative proportion of women continues to grow.

As regards crude death rates (CDRs), the ratio of deaths in a specified period to the average total population in

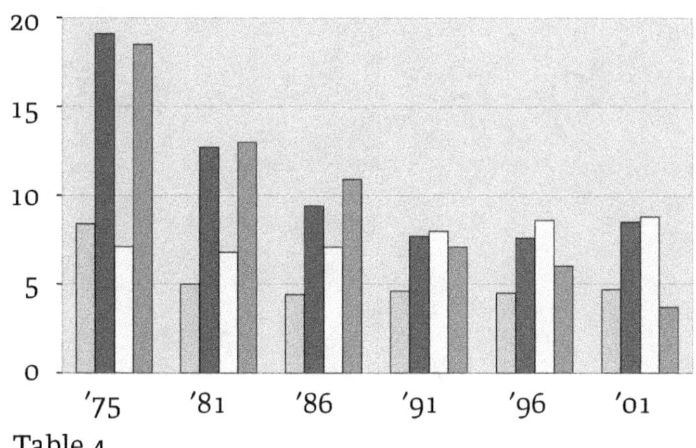

Table 4

	Gross Rates (%)				Life Expectancy at Birth	
	CMR	CBR	CDR	IMR	Men	Women
1975	8.4	19.1	7.1	18.5	69.6	76.9
1981	5.0	12.7	6.8	13.0	71.0	78.5
1986	4.4	9.4	7.1	10.9	72.4	79.7
1991	4.6	7.7	8.0	7.1	72.8	81.5
1996	4.5	7.6	8.6	6.0	74.2	82.4
2001	4.7	8.5	8.8*	3.7	73.3**	82.7**

Evolution of marriage (cmr)
The dramatic decline of both the crude marriage rate and, concomitantly, the crude birth rate between 1975 and 2001 accelerated the tendency toward an older population in the Basque Autonomous Community. As the population progressively aged, there also emerged a noteworthy difference in life expectancy levels according to gender.
*Source: EUSTAT (The Basque Institute of Statistics) and INE (The National Statistics Institute): * in 2000 and ** in 1998.*

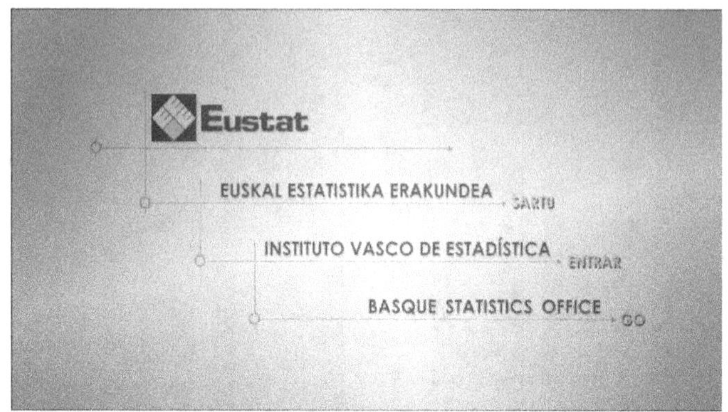

The importance of statistics
EUSTAT, the Basque Institute of Statistics. This organization constructs and shows Basque society through the medium of the Internet using a large database. The demographic section of the database is especially important.

---

that period, they rose from 7.1 deaths per thousand inhabitants in 1975 to 8.8 in 2000. This increase should not, however, be interpreted as a decline in standards of living or a rising mortality as the result of one specific reason, but rather as the direct consequence of an ageing population. Between 1975 and 1996, the life expectancy at birth in the Basque Autonomous Community rose for both women and men. In 1996, it was 82.4 for females and 74.2 for males. As regards the infant mortality rate (IMR), the number of deaths during a specified period of live-born infants who have not reached their first birthday, divided by the number of the live births in the period, it is less than ten per thou-sand, and its progressive decline is a clear sign of generally good development levels and health standards.

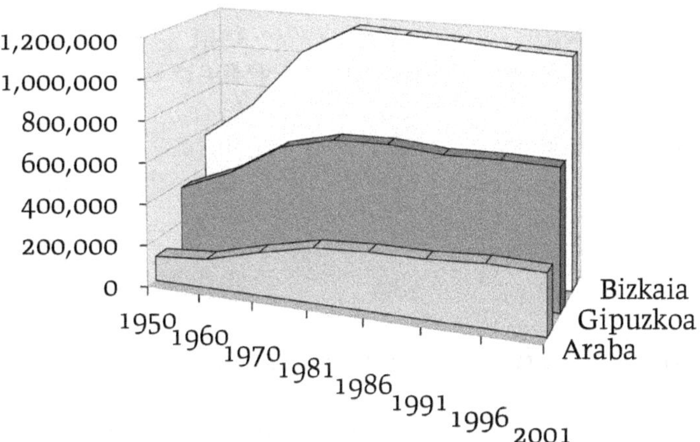

Table 7

	Araba	**Bizkaia**	**Gipuzkoa**
1950	118,012	569,188	374,040
1960	138,934	754,383	478,337
1970	204,323	1,043,310	631,003
1981	260,580	1,181,401	692,986
1986	275,703	1,168,405	698,894
1991	276,457	1,156,245	676,307
1996	291,615	1,135,657	680,035
2001	286,387	1,122,637	673,563

Evolution of the population in Araba, Gipuzkoa, and Bizkaia, 1950–2001
There was a dramatic population growth in the three historic territories between 1950 and 1970, but thereafter, between 1970 and 2001, only Araba maintained significant growth levels, with Bizkaia and Gipuzkoa suffering population declines in the same period.
Source: EUSTAT (The Basque Institute of Statistics) and INE (The National Statistics Institute).

Table 6

	TNR (Women)* (%)	MAM (Women)*	TNR (Men)* (%)	MAM (Men)*
1975	93.3	24.2	99.7	26.7
1981	64.1	24.3	66.9	26.6
1986	51.6	25.0	52.7	28.6
1991	56.1	27.0	54.5	29.4
1996	54.7	28.5	52.5	30.8

Evolution of the total marriage rate among Women and Men

Between 1975 and 2001, a significant change took place in marriage patterns in the Basque Autonomous Community. Increasingly, fewer people got married, and those who did married progressively later in life than in previous generations.

*Source: EUSTAT (The Basque Institute of Statistics) *in 1975–76, 1980–81, 1985–86, 1990–91, and 1995–96.*

TRANSFORMATIONS IN THE FAMILY

IN RECENT decades in Europe, the processes that configure the family have undergone great changes. The result has been important adjustments both in the process of family formation and the resulting family structures. These changes have been so significant that some observers have even spoken of a second demographic transition, following the aging of the population. One should highlight, among other things, decreasing marriage rates, falling fertility rates, the appearance of new, noninstitutionalized forms of relationships (such as cohabitation), an increase in extramarital births, and a rising divorce rate. These changes, which in the most

Into the mouth of Gargantúa
A metaphor of the aging process? Gargantúa (the Gargantuan), a popular attraction, literally swallows up the children who enter his mouth.
Photo: Iñaki Martínez de Albeniz.

advanced countries began to take place in the 1960s, came later to the BAC, but with an unusual intensity.

There have been important changes in both the structure and organization of fertility, and these in turn imply transformations in family organization. During the last quarter of the twentieth century, fertility rates have slowed down. In 1975–76, the average fecundity rates for the time (as represented by the total fertility rate, or TFR, the number of children a woman or man would have during a lifetime if she or he were to experience the fertility rates of the period at each age of an individual's reproductive life) were well above the basic replacement level (2.7 babies per female and 2.6 per male). In 1995–96, these fell to below this same level (0.9 babies for both females and males). Furthermore, average maternity and paternity ages rose considerably, with the result that in 1996 (on average) women became mothers at the age of 31.3, while men became fathers at the age of 33.8. One clear reflection of these changes in the structure of the family is the proportional rise of extramarital births: While in 1975 only 1.4 percent of births took place outside of marriage, in 2001, this figure rose to 16.3 percent. This growth in extramarital fertility was the direct consequence of transformations taking place in couple formation and, more specifically, in the growing number of cohabiting couples. Different studies confirm that, for the most part, these births took place within de facto relationships and were not the result of unknown or absent fathers.

ONE SHOULD also take note of changes in legal regulations regarding the family between 1978 and 1981. These changes stemmed from new governing principles regarding family life in the 1978 Spanish Constitution and the 1981 reform of the Civil Code. As regards the institution of marriage, these implied the recognition of the equality of both spouses; the possibility of undertaking either a civil or church marriage, indiscriminately and without the need for any sort of subsequent authorization; and the right to divorce. As regards progeny, these changes established an equality of rights among children, whether born within or outside marriage.

MARRIAGE RATES

THE EVOLUTION of nuptiality or marriage rates can also be examined in the same way. Between 1975 and 2001 the total nuptiality rate (TNR), the number of women or men of a cohort who would marry during their lifetime if they were to experience the nuptiality rates of the period at each age, fell by almost half. How might this be explained? If a whole generation followed 1975 Basque marriage patterns, almost all women (93.3 percent) and all men (99.7 percent) would end up getting married. That is, 1975 marked a period of high marriage rates. On the other hand, if this same generation followed the 1996 marriage pattern, just over half the people (54.7 percent of women and 52.5 percent of men) would get married. This fall in marriage rates was accompanied by a growth in the mean age at marriage (MAM), the average age at which individuals marry, with the result that both women and men got married, on average, four years later in 2001 than in 1975.

The proportion of second and civil marriages also grew, although these second marriages never rose above 5 percent of the total and civil ones 30 percent. One should also point out the rising divorce rate, together with more and more second unions featuring divorced women and, especially, divorced men.

MIGRATORY MOVEMENTS

Migration is undoubtedly a more complex phenomenon to assess than changes in the family. As mentioned above, migratory movements were extremely important in the general population growth between 1950 and 1975, then took a negative turn after 1981. In other words, more people began to leave the BAC than to settle there after this latter date. Quantitatively speaking, then, the most relevant negative migratory statistics date from the 1980s and were a direct consequence of the industrial crisis at that time.

Taking account of the importance of this phenomenon in shaping the political and social characteristics of the BAC (see Section 1, Chapter 1), it is worth considering the effect of migration on each historic territory. As the data demonstrate, between 1950 and 1970, Bizkaia received the greatest number of people (most of whom settled mainly in Greater Bilbao), followed by Gipuzkoa (where the population was distributed among many centers) and Araba. After 1970, Bizkaia, where the industrial crisis had its greatest effect, grew less quickly than the other historic territories. And after 1981, Araba was the only one of the three that didn't actually lose people, a phenomenon linked to the naming of Vitoria (its capital) as the capital of the BAC.

In recent years, foreign immigration has become the dominant theme of European demography, relegating worries about fecundity to a secondary level. In this respect, one should point out the relative lack of importance of this phenomenon in the BAC: it accounted for only 1.5 per cent of the total population in 2001, or thirty thousand people, of whom three out of every four came from outside the European Union. To judge by the statistics, EUSTAT gives more importance to interior than to foreign migrations, and should one wish to obtain more information about the foreign population, it is better to consult the INE database.

EDUCATIONAL LEVELS

Until well into the twentieth century, access to education was defined by social status and gender, with very few people (and only those, in a sense, economically preselected) achieving an educational level beyond the primary stage. However in the last thirty years, since the 1970 General Law of Education, education has been more accessible and has improved in both quality and variety, leading to a important transformation in its social significance.

BROADLY SPEAKING, one might argue that the educational level has improved perceptively with the disappearance of illiterate and uneducated people from the population as a whole and with a significant reduction in the level of those people with only primary-level education. Moreover, although among older generations, men were better educated than women, today, among the youngest generations, the situation has been reversed, with the result that women outnumber men as a percentage in higher education.

Lesson three

LEARNING OBJECTIVES

1. To identify the principal demographic phenomena.
2. To understand the basic information regarding the demographic evolution of the Basque Autonomous Community between 1975 and 2001.
3. To relate demographic phenomena to both socioeconomic development and population studies.

4. To understand the characteristics and importance of migratory movements in the Basque Country from the 1950s to the present.

REQUIRED READING

Begoña Arregi, "Women's Position and Fertility in the Peninsular Basque Country," in *Eusko Ikaskuntza, Cuadernos de sección: Historia-Geografía* 22 (1994): 393–412.

Begoña Arregi, and Isabel Larrañaga, "On the Reproduction of the Basque Family," *Sociological Abstracts*, Abstracts of the 14th World Congress of Sociology, Montreal, July 26–August 1, 1998, vol. 1 (Montreal: International Sociological Association, 1998), 19.

SUGGESTED READING

It would be a good idea to visit the following databases to obtain information about the demographic evolution of the Basque Country: EUSTAT (www.eustat.es), INE (www.ine.es), and the Centre d'Estudis Demogràficas (www.ced.uab.es).

WRITTEN LESSON FOR SUBMISSION

1. Choose a country you are familiar with and compare its demographic evolution to that of the Basque Autonomous Community, using demographic data and information. Use the Population Reference Bureau database (www.prb.org), which has demographic information for almost every country in the world.
2. Make a detailed account of birth, death, and migration rates in the Basque Autonomous Community during the period from 1975 to 2001 using data complementary to that offered here.

Benjamín Tejerina

4 · Linguistic structure

SUMMARY

This chapter analyzes the presence and distribution of the Basque language, Euskara, in the Basque Country by examining data regarding its use and social status, together with an analysis of its structure and distribution: the level of understanding by age, region, and historic territory; the nature of its current use; and aspects related to the promotion of Euskara

BECAUSE it is important to understand not only what the Basque Country *is*, but also how it is *represented*, one can't ignore the plethora of data regarding knowledge of Euskara among Basques. The language has become for many the basic marker of Basque difference, and the work of statistically measuring it—especially the work of sociology—has helped to objectify this conclusion, that is, to convert into a social fact with a shared confirmation.

MEASURING EUSKARA SOCIOLOGICALLY

The first sociological studies to employ quantitative analysis of the state of Euskara appeared around 1970, at the dawn of the Spanish transition to democracy. The first systematic inquiry, however, was undertaken by the Basque Autonomous Government's sociological research think tank in 1982. At that time, the work that best reflected the linguistic situation was the *Atlas lingüístico vasco* (Basque linguistic atlas), and thereafter the information provided by the Electoral Register, the Population and Public Housing Censuses, and sociolinguistic maps.

Here we will examine the social position of Euskara between 1981 and 2001, then analyze the current visibility and use of Euskara and Basque attitudes toward the promotion of Euskara.

THE SOCIAL POSITION OF THE LANGUAGE, 1981–2001

In 2001, there were 656,980 Basque speakers in the Basque Autonomous Community, representing 32.21 percent of the total population. Of these, 527,771 could read and write in the language. Furthermore, some 470,124 people (23.1 percent of the population) spoke some Basque or had some knowledge of Euskara. Finally, half the population, or 906,143 people, had no knowledge of the language at all. The fact that 302,487 people were also quasi-literate Basque speakers indicated that many people were studying Euskara, but had not yet acquired an adequate command of the language. Finally, there were 74,855 passive Basque speakers who, although understanding Euskara to a certain extent, never used it at all.

GEOGRAPHICAL DISTRIBUTION

ARABA HAD the lowest number of Basque speakers: 45,312 people, or one in seven inhabitants in the historic territory, while 165,241 inhabitants, or 59.1 percent of the population, were not bilingual (that is, did not speak Basque). At the same time, Bizkaia had 273,872 Basque speakers, or 24.9 percent of the territory's total population, while there were 551,382 people who did not speak Basque, or 50.2 percent of the population. Gipuzkoa possessed the highest percentage of bilingual people, with just over half the population there speaking Basque (337,796 inhabitants). Indeed, there were more Basque speakers in Gipuzkoa than in Araba and Bizkaia combined: 51.4 percent of all Basque speakers were found there. Just under one-third of the population in Gipuzkoa (189,520) had no knowledge of Euskara.

The areas with the fewest Basque speakers were most of Araba, Greater Bilbao, and western Bizkaia, where figures barely reached 20 percent of the population. Areas with moderate numbers of Basque speakers were northern Araba, western coastal and east-central parts of Gipuzkoa, and central Bizkaia. Finally, the areas with the most Basque speakers were central-coastal and interior parts of Gipuzkoa and eastern-coastal parts of Bizkaia.

THE GENERATIONAL DYNAMIC OF EUSKARA

Linguistic change occurs at a very slow rate. Indeed, language experts generally agree that such variation can be observed only over long periods and that the fate of a language depends, in part, on its capacity to be transmitted from one generation to another.

AS REGARDS the generational growth of Euskara, 25.12 percent of those surveyed born prior to the outbreak of the Spanish Civil War in 1936 were Basque speakers, with this figure rising to 28.2 percent for those of seventy-five years of age and older. This percentage grew still further as the age of the group rose, while for those between sixty and seventy-five years of age, it fell, although still remaining significant: 25.58 percent of those aged between seventy and seventy-five years old spoke Basque, 23.36 percent of those between sixty-five and sixty-nine years of age, and 21.52 percent of those between sixty and sixty-four years of age. This fall in the percentages of Basque speakers was due to the rising population in the Basque Country as a result of migration there during the period of intensive industrialization between the 1950s and early 1970s, a fall in the transmission of the language as a mother tongue in the

Multiplicity of messages
A wealth of communication strategies convey multiple messages in Basque society. Within this communications system, a complex dynamic between state, region and locality, as well as between conventional and unconventional media, compete to articulate these messages. *Photo: PhotoDisc, Inc.*.

second third of the twentieth century, and the arrival of this later generation at adulthood.

One in every three inhabitants between twenty-five and fifty-nine years of age was a Basque speaker, a greater proportion than in the older generation. Within this general range, the older the subgroup, the lower the percentage of Basque speakers, with those between fifty-five and fifty-nine years of age possessing the lowest rate at 21 percent. The migration factor is also important in explaining this low figure, as well, together with the social and political repression of Euskara during the Franco regime (1939–75), which resulted in its banishment from both the public and the educational spheres.

However, the percentages of adults between twenty-five and thirty-nine years of age speaking Basque constantly and gradually increased, from 26 percent to 34 percent. This might be the result of the role played by the *ikastola* movement, in which grade-school or high-school instruction is carried out in Basque, which started in the late 1950s and grew steadily to accommodate 160 schools and more than thirty-three thousand students by 1975 (see Section 3, Chapter 14). If one adds to this a certain painful awareness of the plight of Euskara toward the end of Franco's rule, the beginning of a more positive appraisal of the language, and its introduction into adult education, one might begin to explain the reasons behind the growing recuperation of the Basque language.

The youngest generation today is undergoing an unprecedented linguistic transformation. Those under twenty-four years of age speak Basque at a rate (53.6 percent) double that of those aged seventy-five and over—until recently, the age group with the highest percentage of Basque speakers. Thus, one can say that young adults doubled the Basque-speaking level of their parents' generation, and young children between five and nine years of age (at six out of ten) doubled that of their grandparents' generation.

FAMILY TRANSMISSION OF EUSKARA

In 2001, 502,635 people, or almost one in four inhabitants of the Basque Autonomous Community, claimed Euskara as their mother tongue. Of these, 51.6 percent were women and 48.4 percent were men. In Araba, there were 16,956 mother-tongue Basque speakers, or one in twenty inhabitants; in Bizkaia, 190,002, or 16.9 percent, 52 percent of whom were women and 48 percent men; and in Gipuzkoa, 259,677, or 43.9 percent, 51.3 percent of whom were women and 48.7 percent men.

If one looks at the geographical distribution of these statistics, one sees that 3.3 percent of native Basque speakers lived in Araba, 37.8 percent in Bizkaia, and 58.89 percent in Gipuzkoa. In recent years, however, one can point to 154,345 new Basque speakers (known as *euskaldunberris*)—people who did not grow up with Euskara as their mother tongue.

LINGUISTIC MOBILITY

Such changes in the Basque Country can be measured through linguistic mobility: the losses and gains attributed to different languages. A language may lose speakers as a result of the fact that some people either forget it or stop using it as a means of communication in a set linguistic code. If this loss is continuous and new speakers are not incorporated, one could argue that the language is in a clear process of decline.

THE PROGRESS of Euskara's linguistic mobility during the last fifteen years has been markedly positive. While the percentage of Basque speakers has remained about the same and that of bilingual people has slightly risen, within the group of new Basque speakers, or

Urban and rural
One of the axes along which Basque society can be observed and interpreted is that of urban-rural spaces. This appears as a key means of distinguishing different features of society such as demographic trends, language use and social practices.
Illustration: Seymour Chwast.

euskaldunberris, and, although less relevant from a linguistic point of view, that of partial new Basque speakers, there has been a major transformation. The growth of new Basque speakers has taken place throughout the Basque Country, although it has been especially significant in the three capitals of Bilbao, Vitoria, and San Sebastián, together with several towns on Greater Bilbao's left bank, such as Baracaldo, Santurce, Sestao, and Portugalete, and medium-sized urban centers such as Errenteria and Tolosa in Gipuzkoa and Durango in Bizkaia, as well as throughout the historic territory of Araba.

THE VISIBILITY AND USE OF EUSKARA

The use of Euskara shows features that are the same as or similar to what is exhibited in its role as a mother tongue: It is used more where there are more native Basque speakers. In 2001 in the Basque Country, 286,092 people, 14 percent of the overall population, or two out of every three people who had the language as a mother tongue, said they spoke Euskara at home. Furthermore, 178,663 people used both Spanish and Basque—8.5 percent of the population, or more than double the number of those people who have both languages as mother tongues. If one takes into account all those who claim to speak Basque at home, whether exclusively or together with Spanish, one sees that more than nine out of ten people who have Euskara as a mother tongue use it domestically. On the other hand, 73 percent of all Basque speakers, whether or not they have the language as a mother tongue, speak it at home.

THE POPULATION Census does not cover the different situations in which people use a certain language, but this was addressed by several sociolinguistic surveys between 1991 and 1996. A total of 3,495 Basque speakers were interviewed about their linguistic habits in three areas: in the home and family life, at work and in the nearby environment, and in different day-to-day situations.

THE USE OF EUSKARA IN THE FAMILY

The frequency with which people used Euskara at home ranged from 48 percent, who said they always (or almost always) used the language in certain domestic situations, to 74 percent, who used it to speak to their children. Other situations covered in the interviews reveal the following statistics: 48 percent used Euskara to speak to their grandparents, 51 percent to their partners, 53 percent to their fathers, 56 percent to their mothers, and 59 percent to their siblings. Three out of ten people surveyed declared that preferably they communicated with relatives in Spanish.

THE USE OF EUSKARA IN THE NEARBY ENVIRONMENT

The use of Basque in the workplace, among friends, and in the local community followed the same pattern as that of family use, although at a reduced level. Basque speakers always or nearly always spoke in Basque with friends 50 percent of the time, 45 percent with workmates, 46 percent with senior colleagues, in 48 percent of cases with retailers, and 78 percent in the market.

THE SAME situation was repeated in linguistic exchange in stores, ranging from 86 percent of Basque use in areas where there existed a virtual social bilingualism to 90 percent of Spanish use in areas where there were few bilingual people. In areas where bilingualism was more than 45 percent, Basque tended to predominate over Spanish in the workplace during conversations with workmates and senior colleagues (64 percent and 59 percent, respectively). Only the public space of the market showed a predominance of Basque over Spanish, this in areas where bilingualism was 20 percent or more.

THE USE OF EUSKARA IN FORMAL INTERACTIONS

There have been no systematic studies of the presence of Euskara in more formal situations, although there is data concerning the most frequent everyday functions, such as going to the bank, to the doctor, to city hall, and so on. Here also, Basque speakers usually speak Basque, with the exception of talking to the doctor. Three out of every four Basque speakers use Euskara when talking to their priests, one out of every two at the bank, 59 percent at the city hall, 85 percent with their children's teachers, and one in three when they go to a health center.

The greatest percentages of Basque use in such formal situations are found in areas with 80 percent or more Basque speakers, and these percentages fall in data for areas with fewer bilingual people.

BASQUE ATTITUDES TOWARD THE PROMOTION OF EUSKARA

QUESTIONS about popular attitudes toward measures for helping Basque have been raised since the early 1980s. A majority of people have consistently demonstrated their support for measures that help to encourage the use of Euskara in the education system, public administration, and the media. According to the Basque government publication *La continuidad del Euskera II* (cited as a suggested reading below),

> the measures that receive most support are those aimed at stimulating Basque among the very young, followed by its introduction into public administration and the media. Moreover, one out of every two citizens maintains that they are totally or partially opposed to

> the statement, "I prefer to learn English before learning or improving my Basque." Asked about the linguistic model that they would prefer for their children within the education system, the majority of people in the Basque Autonomous Community (82 percent) chose the bilingual or Basque-only model.

As regards attitudes toward promoting its use, 14 percent declared themselves to be very in favor, 32 percent in favor, 38 percent neither in favor nor against, 14 percent against, and 2 percent very against. Half the people, then, were broadly in favor, while the other half was divided between not having a defined stance toward the issue or being against it.

Lesson four

LEARNING OBJECTIVES

1. To be able to locate the most and least Basque-speaking areas on a map.
2. To comprehend and arrange the most relevant statistical data regarding the number and quality of Basque speakers and Spanish speakers in the contemporary Basque Country.
3. To understand the varied social situations that a minority language experiences.
4. To know some of the reasons why the position of Euskara has improved during recent times.

REQUIRED READING

Joshua A. Fishman, *Language and Ethnicity in Minority Sociolinguistic Perspective* (Clevedon, England: Multilingual Matters, 1989).

Benjamín Tejerina, "Language and Basque Nationalism: Collective Identity, Social Conflict, and Institutionalization," in *Nationalism and the Nation in the Iberian Peninsula: Competing and Conflicting Identities*, ed. Clare Mar-Molinero and Angel Smith (Oxford: Berg, 1996), 221–36.

SUGGESTED READING

Gobierno Vasco, *II Encuesta sociolingüística de Euskal Herria 1996: La continuidad del Euskera II* (Vitoria: Servicio Central de Publicaciones del Gobierno Vasco, 1999).

Benjamín Tejerina, *Nacionalismo y lengua: Los procesos de cambio lingüístico en el País Vasco* (Madrid: CIS-Siglo XXI, 1992).

WRITTEN LESSON FOR SUBMISSION

1. Taking account of the data presented here, what led to the decline and later recuperation of Euskara?
2. Given the data at your disposal about the use of Euskara, explain how the following social institutions have influenced linguistic change: the family, the school, the government.

Section 2: Social mechanisms and institutions

Ignacio Irazuzta

5 · The family

SUMMARY

The family is the primary socialization agent, transforming its new members into social beings. This chapter highlights the family's main general characteristics and the changes that the family has undergone during the modern era so that the particularities of the Basque case can be examined. By means of a brief historical overview, it will explore the importance of the family to Basque nationalist discourse as one example of the traumatic change implied by the advent of modernity in the Basque Country. Finally, the chapter will situate the topic within the process of disparate modernization that occurred during the Franco dictatorship, when changes in the economic sphere did not translate into a concomitant political renovation. The role of the family in ideological reproduction during this period stood out, as it has done since, in the current process of the "privatization of social life."

THE THEME of the family has been extremely important for social thought throughout history. In philosophy, thinkers from Aristotle to G. W. F. Hegel established a tradition in which the family was presented as the basic nucleus from which the rise of larger social entities such as the state could be explained. Anthropology, through its detailed research into family relationships, also has attempted to locate there the genesis of more complex social groupings. Thus, to the present day there has been a tendency to consider the family as the social location closest to nature, as the first instance of contact between an individual and society. Perhaps for this reason, most experts generally regard the family group as one of the most universal of all institutions. However, despite this general agreement, historical diversity and the nature of social change have kept a debate going about framing a characterization for each temporal period or specific cultural reality.

THE FAMILY AS AN AGENT OF SOCIALIZATION

For most modern academic disciplines, the family group was one of the basic themes during the nineteenth and twentieth centuries. The evolutionist nature of theories by the likes of Lewis H. Morgan, Herbert Spencer, Friedrich Engels, and Émile Durkheim led them to try and discover in primitive societies the embryonic form of the modern family. However, the subsequent rejection of these theories led to an increasing emphasis on transformations in family structure, its reduced size, changes in marriage patterns, growing levels of work outside the home, and other factors associated with a more general social and political change within society as a whole. As a result, these more functionalist approaches emphasized family functions (especially sexual, procreative, and socializing ones, together with those of economic cooperation) within the broader social system. Now most experts generally agree that it is impossible to attribute to the family a specific number of special functions and thus to define or espouse a particular theory about it.

THIS CHAPTER will concentrate on the family's socializing function and what this reveals about the more general social structure. The family is a primary agent in the process by which an individual (as a new member of society) adapts to society's requirements. The term "socialization" thus alludes to something akin to learning, to the formation of a personality and the formation within individuals of the main cultural values and norms of a particular society. In its primary phase, it indicates a shift from nature to culture to the extent that the ne w individual is considered a tabula rasa or biological being who, through a series of agents, acquires a social personality.

IN ADDITION to this primary role of the family in the socialization process (a favorite aspect of psychological inquiry), the institution of the family also fulfills a socializing role during the stage closest to adulthood in an individual's life. Sociologists have proposed the concept of political socialization in making reference to the transmission of values associated with the political culture of a society, locating a network of information and symbolic universes that shape an individual's attitudes about and assessments of political institutions. In this way, Anthony Giddens has emphasized how one of the essential values for the successful running of a modern democracy—for example, the concept of individual autonomy—originates in the intimate sphere and especially in the relationship between parents and children.[2]

THE FAMILY IN MODERN SOCIETIES

Approaches that take the family to be the basic nucleus of society have until recently tended to see the family as free of historical change or spatial variation. However, the structure of daily family life, together with its relation to the social structure of contemporary Western societies, came into place only with the birth of the modern world. In modernity, the study of the family, and in more general terms the study of relationships in general, became an essential element in analyzing social structure. As we have noted, this has tended to undermine the assumption of a universal, ahistorcal family structure unaffected by contingencies of time and place. In 1959, within this context, Talcott Parsons discovered a

Rural past
A typical baserri, or Basque farmstead. This represented the traditional family-based economic model and housed extended families.
Photo: Iñaki Martínez de Albeniz.

---

special relationship structure that was urban and bourgeois in the most advanced capitalist country of all: the United States.

ONE OF THE fundamental changes that occurred in the modern era with the advent of capitalist economies was that economic production was no longer limited to the domestic sphere. From now on, home and workplace became different and separate spheres and, as a result, work and family functions began to assume different values and norms. For example, while in the workplace an instrumental rationality guided by calculation and free of affective sentiment predominated, the family space was one of intimacy, romantic and fraternal love, and, in general, characterized by a special relationship guided by a kind of affective rationality. This organizational format of bourgeois society, in turn shaped gender roles, with the woman, as wife-mother, assuming the role of the basic pillar of the domestic sphere and the bearer of its values, while the husband-father concentrated on establishing the basic rules and operated in the work sphere.

JÜRGEN HABERMAS has reconstructed the sequences in this process, demonstrating the development of different spheres of reality in modern societies. The relations of production are made up of the social (private) sphere, differentiated from an earlier intimate one (that of domestic family relations), as well as from another public, or more accurately, political sphere in which the bourgeoisie deliberates on social matters.[3] In the process of modernization, capitalism takes over more traditional forms of production, accentuating the differentiation between the private and public spheres, and relationship associations gradually lose prominence or progressively retire into the private sphere. However this growing tendency toward a concentration in the private sphere leads to the family being considered a key institution for understanding relations between the public and the private and the social and the personal in modern societies.

FAMILY LIFE IN THE BASQUE COUNTRY

In the case of European societies, the family has often acted as prism through which to analyze differences between northern and southern societies. A recurring explanatory argument employs the distinction between regions that have developed a "strong" system of family organization (mainly those in southern Europe) and regions (mainly in the north) where such organization is "weak." In the former case, it is a question of the predominance of the family group over the individual, while in the latter, it is the individual that enjoys a greater social and political role.[4] Proponents of this approach base their reasoning on the degree of Roman or Islamic influence on the continent: That is, while Mediterranean societies display strong family systems, Nordic and Anglo-Saxon areas evince weak family systems.[5]

THE DISTINCTION between the conjugal or nuclear family, shaped according to the principle of divisible inheritances, and the stem family, where one sole heir receives most of the possessions in exchange for remaining with the parents, however, has been the most typical classification for explaining basic European familial systems and their consequences for the social structure. Although there has been a tendency to identify strong family systems with the stem model and greater individualism with the nuclear model, other observers have given more priority to a "strong-versus-weak" model.

THE FAMILY AND BASQUE NATIONALIST DISCOURSE

The generally agreed existence of a stem family model in the Basque Country has been one of the principal historical ingredients in shaping Basque nationalist discourse. Manuel González Portilla and José Urrutikoetxea[6] point out how, that from the early nineteenth century onward, Basque intellectuals such as Juan Antonio de Zamacola underscored the relationship between the family and the foral system. Such intellectuals further alluded to the risk of social disintegration and cultural loss (expressed eloquently in the legal framework of society) that would

New families
The institutionalization of intimacy and new kinds of families. In 2003, it became legal for homosexual couples to adopt children in the Basque Autonomous Community. This decision of the BAC was initially declared unconstitutional, but later was endorsed by the Spanish Parliament.
Photo: Gehitu, the Basque Organization of Gays and Lesbians.

result from the division of property as a result of what was, at the time, seen as the imminent breakup of the stem family. Indeed, for the French sociologist Frédéric Le Play, this family system became the object of a conservative form of sociology that took up a position against the liberal revolutions of the age, declaring them responsible for the loss of traditional forms of social organization. Other works examine this discourse of this causal reconstruction between the family and Basque social organization in some depth. Juan Aranzadi, for example, sees in this discourse an argument linking property forms with "essential" signs of identity that run from the home through to the nation, including surnames and even race. Following this argument, such historical elements as those found in the Basque stem family structure came to shape the plot of a story idealizing the past in making it an archetypal form of Basqueness.

At this initial moment, the references of these intellectuals to the system of family organization were focused on emphasizing a structure and socioeconomic relations based on creating an inheritance. Later, they would ideologically link a whole sociopolitical system to this system of family units. As a consequence, a number of Basque nationalist arguments emerged embracing an antiliberal and anti-industrial element, revealing the trauma of traditional societies confronting modernity for the first time.

THE RISE of economic modernity in the Basque Country, marked by a capitalist industrial economy and workforce, together with the concentration of populations in urban areas of similar size (See Section 1, Chapter 1), brought with it a profound alteration of family organization systems. In particular, the notable and increasing emphasis on the stem family model in Basque nationalist discourse actually revealed the existence of new and different family systems more adapted to industrial development and, therefore, characterized by a lifestyle adapted to the rise of a social milieu different from that of the purely domestic sphere.

HOWEVER, despite this process of modernization, the Basque family continues to be an essential agent of political socialization in the Basque Country. José María Tápiz has demonstrated how Basque nationalism, and especially that of the Basque Nationalist Party (Partido Nacionalista Vasco, PNV) during the Second Spanish Republic (1931–36), managed to plant deep roots in society through strategies of ideological transmission based on a model of the family environment.[7] The party's membership structure often encouraged activities such as debates, meetings, and the like in spaces especially apt for family gatherings (including special bars or restaurants affiliated to the party, known as *batzokis*), in effect creating its collective political base. Furthermore, the discovery of family ties between party members served to emphasize that such an environment was of considerable importance in transmitting party doctrine. Tápiz even suggests that this ideological transmission within the family structure was one of the factors that kept Basque nationalism going during the Franco dictatorship, as well as aiding its powerful resurgence during the later reinstatement of democracy. Finally, he also points out that this form of generating support within the PNV encouraged, through senior members or their descendants, many of the political organizations that emerged or were developed during the period of political normalization in the Spanish state after Franco's death in 1975.

THE FAMILY DURING THE FRANCO DICTATORSHIP

As a result of the strict control of public spaces during the Franco dictatorship (1939–75), ideological and cultural reproduction withdrew into the private sphere, and the family took on an especially important role. Significantly, and parallel to this phenomenon, the intimate sphere was also charged with reproducing Euskara, banned at that time from all public spaces (see Section 2, Chapter 10). Thus, a solid intersubjective network contributed to the emergence of a critical Basque nationalist consciousness that gradually came to support the violence of ETA (Euskadi 'ta Askatasuna, Basque Homeland and Liberty) and that concomitantly came to reject the violence of the state, expressed through its security forces. This ideological support was expressed as a form of affective rationality that characterized intimate social spaces such as those of family or friendship relations. One should highlight the fact that this intersubjective form of a slowly growing political support came about in the context of a society with a high degree of industrial and urban development and that this sociological portrait of the Basque Country during the Franco dictatorship reveals a contradiction with the typical picture of differentiated spheres of reality that are supposed to function in industrial societies, where the family assumes functions outside the public realm. The impossible nature of undertaking politics in rational terms (a basic characteristic of public life in modern societies) has moved some observers to point out the importance of private spaces such as the family in order to explain the birth and survival of political violence in the Basque Country.[8]

As politics became more open and professional from the mid-1970s onward during the Spanish transition to democracy, this affective form of ideological reproduction declined. Consequently a "growing privatization of social life"[9] took place that tended to relegate the family to the socialization and raising of its youngest members through those means that, like religion, modernity had confined to the private sphere.

Accentuating this process, forms of family life in the contemporary Basque Country (as in any advanced capitalist society) increasingly demonstrate a tendency toward valuing intimate spaces and personal autonomy,[10] which may transform traditional nuclear families, composed of a father, mother, and children, in ways that might require institutional integration. Homosexual couples and especially unmarried de facto partners are more and more common in the Basque Country and herald a tendency toward the growing role of individuals controlling their own lives, as well as toward more official recognition of these developments, as evinced by the social policy of different governmental authorities.

FROM THE nineteenth century onward, then, Basque nationalist discourse linked the special nature of Basque society to its stem family base, while the family served as a basic agent of ideological reproduction during the Franco dictatorship. Today, in light of the contemporary tendency toward framing new family models, the family continues to occupy a central place in Basque intellectual debate. An extensive body of work by social science and an equally prolific cultural production (both in literature and film) highlight, respectively, its continuing importance in the field of social relations and the individual biographies of numerous contemporary Basque artists.

Lesson five

LEARNING OBJECTIVES

1. To understand the sociological relevance of the family through its role as a socialization agent.
2. To relate the family, through its various relationships, to the social structure of the Basque Country.
3. To identify the principal characteristics of the Basque family model.
4. To recognize the main periods of demarcation in the historical sociology of the family in the Basque Country.

REQUIRED READING

Talcott Parsons, "The Social Structure of the Family," in *The Family: Its Function and Destiny*, ed. Ruth Nanda Anshen (New York: Harper and Row, 1949), 173–201.

Carrie Hamilton, "Remembering the Basque Nationalist Family: Daughters, Fathers and the Reproduction of the Radical Nationalist Community," *Journal of Spanish Cultural Studies* 1, no. 2 (2000): 153–71.

SUGGESTED READING

Manuel González Portilla and José Urrutikoetxea, "Familia vasca e historia: Entre el cambio y las resistencias," *Cuadernos del Alzate* 20 (1999): 205–18.

CEIC (Centro de Estudios sobre la Identidad Colectiva), *Institutionalización política y reecantamiento de la socialidad: Las transformaciones del mundo nacionalista, Soziologiako euskal koadernoak / Cuadernos sociológicos vascos, no. 2* (Vitoria: Gobierno Vasco, 1999).

WRITTEN LESSON FOR SUBMISSION

1. Critically describe and discuss the family in the Basque Country on the basis of how it is represented through film in movies such as *Vacas, La Muerte de Mikel,* and so on.
2. Analyze the historical change in the Basque family unit as regards the differentiation of public and private spheres.

Zesar Martínez

6 · The associative world

Cuadrillas and peer groups

SUMMARY

This chapter addresses social relations in another part of the private sphere outside that of the family: those associated with people's leisure time. It examines the formation of large peer groups such as cuadrillas, or large groups of friends, together with the associative-recreational world of txokos, or gastronomic societies, and the respective social practices these produce. It is important to understand this aspect of the social realm because it demonstrates the basic everyday connections and development mechanisms of political identities in the Basque Country. As a result, the topic is closely related to the chapter on youth and social relations. Here, a general description of various groups and associations will highlight their importance to what sociology understands as one of the most important agents of socialization.

THE ASSOCIATIVE world in the Basque Country is thick, active, and varied. It is shaped by different aspects of public and social life: from *cuadrillas*, or large peer groups, and *txokos*, or gastronomic societies—examined in this section—to an endless number of cultural and recreational organizations: dance groups, hiking clubs, leisure groups, fiesta or festival commissions, and looser groups of friends organized into associations to help animate towns and cities during carnival or fiesta time. There are, furthermore, more formal collectives or organizations that work toward specific social, political, or cultural goals: the recovery of the Basque language and culture; ecological and environmental concerns; women's rights; international solidarity and antiglobalization activities; antimilitarism and (previously, before it was abolished)) anticonscription; pacifism and solidarity with the victims of political violence; young people's collectives, *gaztetxes*, or unofficial social centers for young people; antirepressive political prisoners' support groups; collectives against social exclusion; neighborhood associations; and so on. These other groups are addressed in more detail in Chapter 12. However, by listing them here one gets a general overview of the social fabric of Basque society that, as will be seen, is marked by its plural and heterogeneous nature. This is evident in ideological, linguistic, and national identity questions, as well as in socioeconomic stratification and rural or urban environments. *Cuadrillas* and *txokos* will be examined in more detail here, initially through a description of their general characteristics and traditional activities and then via an examination of the changes that have taken place in recent years in these particular forms of interaction and group structuration.

CUADRILLAS AND *POTEO*

THE *CUADRILLA* is one of the most typical forms of interaction and socialization in the Basque Country. It is a large group of people formed according to similarity in age, gender, neighborhood residence, or schooling. They are peer groups in which the number of members varies according to age and geographical origin (urban or rural). The generational factor, however, is the most important determining factor. Typically, in rural areas among the youngest groups (adolescents), *cuadrillas* may have between ten and twenty members, while in urban areas among older people, they have only between five and ten members.

Cuadrillas, according to the most typical traditional definition (which, as will be seen, is not exactly the

Communal sociality
Traditional forms of sociality among peer groups. A group of senior citizens sing bilbainadas (traditional songs from Bilbao) during the city's annual fiesta. *Photo: Iñaki Martínez de Albeniz.*

---

norm among young people today) are usually formed not only by selective bonds of personal friendship or similarity, but also by those previously mentioned socially assigned elements: belonging to a specific age, gender, residential, or school-related group. In this sense, although at the core of the *cuadrilla* there are strong and close relations among some of its members, what generally unites the group is not this kind of connection. Rather, it is more a question of simply belonging to a specific generational group that, through the *cuadrilla*, is linked to the social life of a town or neighborhood.

EFFECTIVELY, the *cuadrilla* allows people to present themselves in collective form as part of a group in the social life of their town or neighborhood, usually in leisure-time activities: simple social interaction (or just "hanging out"), amusement, recreation, fiestas, and so on. As a human group, it is internally structured (as a day-to-day reference for leisure time, the living of common experiences, group involvement, and the like). However, it is also structured, perhaps even most importantly, externally, that is, as a reference point of social public life in its most local, everyday dimension, its informal social and interactive spaces and moments.

To a certain extent, the *cuadrilla* allows individuals to present themselves and to interact not only through their personal identities, but also as members of large groups from which, crucially, they also take part of their own identities: "The significant thing is their applicability ... as a key institution in a certain part of the public environment, with all that this implies for the specific defining of socially acceptable behavior and of elements in the construction of a collective identity code."[11] This is an institution that allows one to live social life collectively in public spaces, bars, or during fiestas and so on. And all of this takes place through a powerful integration and intragroup identification based on nothing more than basic similarity or friendship ties with each and every member of the group. Complicity, affinity, or more personal friendships usually emerge between some members of the *cuadrilla*, but not among everyone. Indeed, more intimate and personal issues don't usually form part of the interaction among the wider group.[12]

Every *cuadrilla* has a public image and implies a collective form of differentiation-addition that produces several routines and interaction norms. The *cuadrilla* decides on places to meet and draws up schedules that are usually ritually set, together with the activities that take place according to the time of day, week, or location. Even without specifically arranging to meet, *cuadrilla* members know where to find their friends at any given time. There are also defined codes, signs, and symbols that mean that being in the *cuadrilla* is an activity in itself. Indeed, this becomes the *natural* activity during leisure time. The *cuadrilla,* in this sense, is assembled as a structure of plausibility, an environment of trust that by its routine and predictability is well disposed to making its members feel happy and relaxed. At the same time, it also serves as a platform or bridge for entering the public social life of a town or neighborhood.

AS REGARDS *cuadrilla* activities, traditionally having a *pote* (literally, a pot or jar, but meaning a drink) or *poteo* is the collective ritual par excellence. Although important changes have taken place in the last fifteen years, *cuadrillas* today still tend to have a handful of bars that they habitually frequent. This is exactly what *poteo* is all about—going from bar to bar having small glasses of wine or beer while at the same time talking with one another and greeting members of other *cuadrillas*, the bartenders, and so forth. In *poteo* there is usually a predefined route to be completed, during which time the larger group divides into smaller ones who regroup later according to different greetings, conversation topics, and so on. *Poteo* bars are usually grouped together in two or three adjacent streets and are frequented in a set order at a relaxed pace. Each *cuadrilla* has its established itinerary that, by its cyclical nature, allows the incorporation of any member even if they haven't arranged to meet beforehand. As a result, a kind of socializing or mixing takes place that is marked by its visibility in the public

Youth socialization

Young people have occupied an old factory in Leioa, Bizkaia, and converted it into a Gaztetxe, or unofficial youth center.
Photo: Iñaki Martínez de Albeniz.

---

sphere, in the central or main streets of towns or neighborhoods. In this way these central or *poteo* areas are usually full of a continuous stream of *cuadrillas* walking around (creating a lively collective or communal atmosphere), typically on the weekend or on holidays from midday until lunchtime (two o'clock onward) and from dusk until dinnertime (ten o'clock onward), Thus, "the streets are swarming with people where the group dynamic—the *cuadrilla*—is obviously in charge of structuring all relations."[13]

Periodic lunches, dinners, or other special celebrations are other especially important activities in the life of a *cuadrilla*. Because they are special events, a great deal of thought and preparation goes into them, and the choice of place and menu (and of gifts or fancy dress that accompany stag parties, for example) are meticulously planned. These events are highly ritualized and serve to reinforce group identity. And of course, participation is very important to the *cuadrilla* members.

Cuadrillas in the Basque Country have been traditionally male, and this is still the case today for those people aged around fifty and over. In fact, the tradition persists today among these groups of men going out with their *cuadrillas* to do *poteo* while women stay at home preparing the lunch or dinner. This relegation of women to outside the most public or visible public sphere is in clear decline, given that younger *cuadrillas* today are usually mixed. Indeed, this has been one of the most significant changes of the last twenty or twenty-five years. Typically today, adolescents form separate *cuadrillas* according to gender that later transform into mixed groups as they become young adults.

BEFORE describing the changes that have taken place in the *cuadrilla* as a social institution in recent times, one should also take note of another special institution in the social life of the Basque Country: the *txokos*, or gastronomic societies.

TXOKOS, OR GASTRONOMIC SOCIETIES

Txokos are groups formed by various *cuadrillas* that purchase or rent a location and create there a specific space to have lunches, dinners, and celebrations. These events usually take place in an atmosphere of gastronomic camaraderie that includes having lively informal group discussions, songs, card games, and so on. The *txokos* are centered on gastronomy and are marked by a nonprofessional organizational model based on the equal division of expenses and responsibilities among all members. They are traditionally male-only groups, and female access to the premises is strictly limited. Although there has been a relaxing of this rule in recent years, even today, women can enter some *txokos* only if accompanied by a man, and not in their own right. Whatever the particular case, the kitchen is the reserved space par excellence for members, due to its unlimited access to the food, the bar, the pantry, the wine cellar, and so on.

The *txoko* has a family atmosphere, somewhat like a second home, where the social control associated with the public sphere (in bars, restaurants, and in the streets) is relaxed or cancelled out altogether. The members themselves provide the food, make the meals, and serve the drinks in a relaxed atmosphere of trust. The whole planning and administering of the *txoko* is carried out amid intragroup trust and unity.

AS A FORM of establishing basic interpersonal relations (by age and gender), these gastronomic societies imply the singling out of a particular space, making it their own through a series of mechanisms associated with communal use and egalitarian organization among all the members. Depending on the town or city where they are located, they may assume a more public dimension during local fiestas or celebrations: the clearest example of this takes place during the *tamborrada* (drum celebration) in San Sebastián, a fiesta basically performed by the gastronomic societies of that city. However, *txokos* are normally very private and particular, with less of a public dimension. They are essential structures of social relations that, in many ways, "impart

---

personality to the collective, presenting it as a social community."[14]

CUADRILLAS AND PEER GROUPS AMONG YOUNGER GENERATIONS

The changes that have affected this particular social institution in generational terms have been so far reaching that it is highly debatable whether one really can apply the *cuadrilla* concept (according to the traditional definition above) to group formation among younger generations today. One might perhaps argue that it is still a concept that has a certain validity and significance in rural environments and among very young groups (adolescents between fourteen and seventeen years of age). However, in cities and among young people aged between eighteen and twenty, it is losing its importance in favor of smaller groups of friends based solely on personal relationships.

ALREADY by the 1980s, and especially compared with the heady decades of the 1960s and 1970s, with their heightened politicization of the social and associative framework of the Basque Country (see Section 3, Chapter 13), there was a marked decline in the importance of the *cuadrilla* as an everyday social institution. For example, the *poteo* custom among *cuadrillas* is now not an everyday ritual, although it is still important on weekends and on the eves of certain holidays. This decline in the frequency of interaction is especially noticeable among younger generations. This is because they do not have as much free time during the week, due to work demands that involve greater spatial mobility and that are more and more demanding and competitive. Also, they tend to use their free time not to "hang out with friends," but rather to do sports, hobbies, or activities associated with complementing their professional lives (learning languages, taking classes, and so on). Leisure time, in this sense, is becoming a more and more occupied, organized, and planned out, a time that must be "made use of" for activities that are, to some extent, constructive or that lead to some measurable personal satisfaction. In this sense, Basque society now displays tendencies resembling those of other Western societies: the privatization of life, individualism, competitiveness, and a weakening of more day-to-day or public group ties. Consequently, one might argue that in the contemporary Basque Country, being with one's *cuadrilla* has ceased to be a natural everyday activity once the working day is finished, although it *is* still a reference point on weekends or on special occasions (during special lunches, dinners, stag parties, and so on).

It is almost certainly this decline in the frequency of interaction that has weakened the most ritualized and defining aspects of the *cuadrilla* as a reference point for group interaction. The profound level of intragroup integration and assimilation based on generational, gender, or neighborly ties described above has been weakened in favor of ties based more on personal friendships. And this has resulted in smaller groups, founded on similar likes and dislikes that only reinforce the personal nature of the relations.

THAT SAID, among adolescents, and especially in the smaller rural towns, the large *cuadrilla* continues to be a platform or bridge toward peer interaction and incorporation into the life of the town or neighborhood. These adolescent and young *cuadrillas* largely occupy the bar area of such places on weekends, especially late at night, although intergroup interaction increasingly takes place not just in bars (the traditional space), but also in quieter public spaces such as squares, parks, and porches.

Cuadrillas and poteo
The rituals of free time and informal associative life in the Basque Country. Here, cuadrillas (large groups of friends) go from bar to bar in the poteo ritual.
Photo: Iñaki Martínez de Albeniz.

FOLLOWING the *txoko* model, in a relatively recent phenomenon, young *cuadrillas* are renting premises to make them into *txoko*-like spaces for their private use and enjoyment. In most cases, these are places (such as garages or unoccupied stores below apartment buildings) that are subsequently furnished (quite sparsely) with whatever they have at hand or can get relatively easily: sofas, a television, a VCR, a PlayStation, a CD player, and a refrigerator, for example. This self-financing and self-regulation, together with the possibility of having their own space beyond the supervision or control of adults, is what makes the phenomenon an important reference point for adolescents, principally in urban areas. It is also significant that its persistence is gradually replacing another form of self-regulation among young people that flourished in the 1980s and early 1990s: the *gaztetxes* or unofficial young people's social centers. These are a phenomenon, however, that still exists today in many towns and cities in the Basque Country and that is marked by a more overtly political and cultural nature: as a center of alternative activities for more socially and politically active young people (see Section 3, Chapter 15).

IN SHORT, the reality of peer groups among young Basques is, today, very plural and heterogeneous in that it contains several different types, spaces, and expressions, depending on variables such as different youth cultures (music, aesthetics, symbolism, and so on), being in a rural or urban environment, and one's age span and/or different ethnolinguistic identity (see Section 3, Chapter 14).

Lesson six

LEARNING OBJECTIVES

1. To understand the sociological importance of peer groups and other associative forms.
2. To understand the main forms and characteristics of the associative world in the Basque Country.
3. To understand the main patterns of change within the associative framework of the Basque Country after the Franco dictatorship.
4. To analyze the implications of the associative world for the political development of the Basque Country.

REQUIRED READING

Sharryin Kasmir, "'More Basque than You': Class, Youth, and Identity in an Industrial Basque Town," *Identities: Global Studies in Culture and Power* 9 (2002): 39–68.

Benjamín Tejerina, "Cycles of Protest, Social Movements and Political Violence in the Basque Country," *Nations and Nationalism* 7, no. 1 (2001): 39–57.

SUGGESTED READING

Jesús Arpal, "Solidaridades elementales y organizaciones colectivas en el País Vasco (cuadrillas, txokos, asociaciones)," in *Processus sociaux, idéologies et pratiques culturelles dans la société basque*, ed. Pierre Bidart (Pau: Université de Pau et des Pays de l'Adour; CNRS, 1985). 129–54.

Kontxesi Berrio-Otxoa, Jone Hernández, and Zesar Martínez, *Haur eta nerabeen aisialdi antolatua Gipuzkoan* (Donostia: Gipuzkoako Foru Aldundia, 2000).

WRITTEN LESSON FOR SUBMISSION

1. Work out a sociological bibliography about peer and friendship groups and, using it as a theoretical baseline, analyze the importance of the *cuadrilla* and *txokos* in the Basque Country.
2. Critically analyze the implications that associative formations have had in the political development of the Basque Country.

Gabriel Gatti

7 · The education system

SUMMAry

In the general framework of socialization in modern societies, the school is one of its most important agents: It guarantees the production and continuity of collective communal sentiment and aids the production of intergenerational consciousness and continuity. In the Basque Country, the relevant authorities have constructed an educational system that produces a shared and legitimate consciousness about Basque identity and about the shared history of the community itself. The status of language, history, and identity are questions raised by the Basque education system, in whose schools subjects of different ethnic, cultural, linguistic, and political backgrounds meet and live together.

THE EDUCATION system in general and the institution of the school in particular are and have been favorite objects of analysis for sociological literature.[15] This is hardly surprising, since both reveal some of the basic issues for sociological inquiry: intragenerational and intergenerational relations, socialization, institutional space, the reproduction of culture, and so on. Moreover, the school itself, a quintessentially modern institution and one directly linked to birth of modern states, is also one of the most important mechanisms for the reproduction and maintenance of consciousness. One might contend that the educational world today constitutes the basic form of social reproduction in modern societies.

Taking account of these considerations, without pretending to be able to cover everything, one might think about the school as a relevant field of study for sociology from two different perspectives. The first considers the school as an institution that performs important functions of social reproduction, that is, as one of the institutions that contributes to perpetuating (or at least to maintaining) a cultural system from generation to generation. Through plans of study—whether concealed or obvious—it intervenes in the learning and reproducing of values, attitudes, and behavioral norms; influences the construction of a common or shared history; and intervenes in the elaboration of a common imaginary space based on a legitimate identity and language. In other words, we are here faced with one of the most important modern socialization agents, one of the places where generational and collective consciousness is shaped.

The second perspective sees the educational sphere in terms of its ecological niche or as an elemental place in everyone's life. The school is also, in this way, an interesting target of research for sociology, since here the school's space-time framework appears as both an institutionalized space that allows one to observe routines of interaction and the ritualization of behavior and as a place of generational reference, where one behaves and through such behavior learns to be a social actor.

IN SUM, it is at school where the social actor first encounters, in the most direct way, the complexities of the public space, knowledge of others, and the construction of his or her own identity. Further, one could also say that the school is a place where one learns, negotiates, and manages collective identity and difference, where, in intergenerational fashion, subjects from different backgrounds learn to live together.

The present chapter will focus on this latter aspect: the school as a space of intercultural negotiation. Although the question of the school in the Basque Country can be and indeed has been approached from the first of

Basque-language schooling in the city
The Abusu ikastola in the La Peña neighborhood, on the outskirts of Bilbao, Bizkaia. In 2001, this was the site of the Ibilaldia, an annual sponsored walk held in different towns and cities to raise funds for Basque-language learning. The day-long event attracted 120,000 people. *Photo: Iñaki Martínez de Albeniz.*

---

these two perspectives (as a socialization agent), it is difficult to highlight in that way any basic differences of the Basque Country from the rest of the world. For this reason, we will focus on the school as a space where different expressions of culture, as language, society, and identity are evinced by students as they live side by side and negotiate with one another. This perspective will allow us to observe a reality that is rich in complexity and interesting for its specific nature.

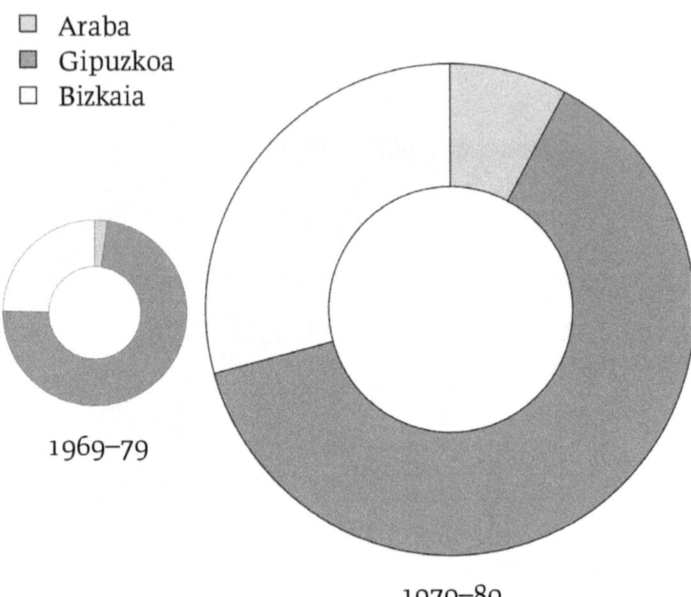

Table 8

Historic Territory	1969–70	1979–80
Araba	171	4,277
Gipuzkoa	5,770	34,733
Bizkaia	1,958	16,136

Enrollment in ikastolas

From modest and semiclandestine beginnings during the Franco dictatorship, enrollment in ikastolas grew significantly with the Basque institutionalization process of the late 1970s. The ikastola phenomenon was generally stronger in the more Basque-speaking territories of Gipuzkoa and Bizkaia than in Araba. *Source: Jesús Arpal, et al.,* Educación y sociedad en el País Vasco *(Donostia: Txertoa, 1982), 89.*

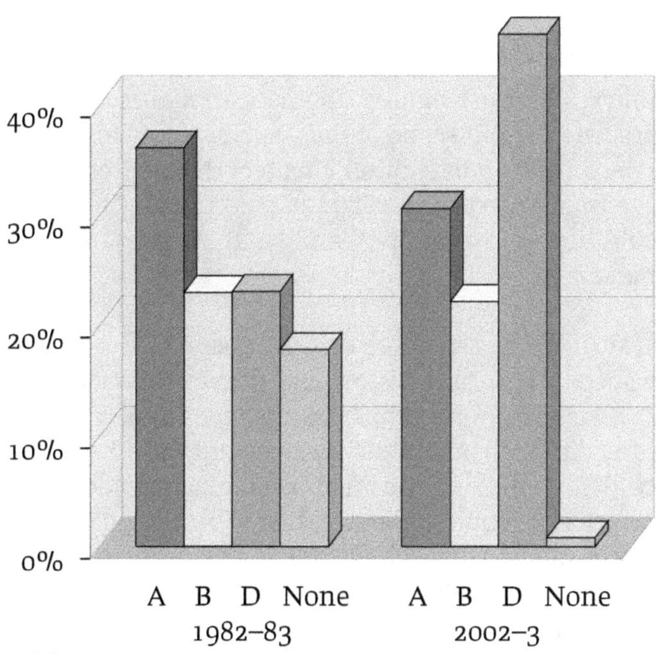

Table 9

Model	1982–83 School year	2002–3 School year
A (Basque as a subject)	36.1%	30.6%
B (Bilingual teaching)	23.0%	22.2%
D (Teaching in Basque)	23.1%	46.4%
No teaching of Basque	17.8%	0.8%

Students according to teaching model
The most significant change in the Basque educational system between the early 1980s and the turn of the century was the progressive growth of enrollment in Model D (all classes taught in Basque), at the expense of an education in Spanish alone (with either Basque as a subject or not taught at all).
Source: Author's calculation from EUSTAT (The Basque Institute of Statistics) data.

The focus here is on how the Basque school reflects some of the conflicts that arise in and affect the Basque Country. These are mainly linguistic in nature, and to appreciate the full scope of the issue, it would also be worth consulting here other chapters that address language issues (Section 1, Chapter 4, Section 2, Chapter 10, and Section 3, Chapter 14,) and youth matters (Section 3, Chapter 15).

THE SCHOOL IN THE BASQUE COUNTRY

The specific nature of history and the education system in the Basque Country must be analyzed in the context of Basque nationalism and its relationship with the central state. School models classified by language predominate, what defines people's identity, history, or language differ according to what school is being analyzed and where it is located in the Basque Country, and the ideological and cultural references that direct the elaboration of the teaching programs there are also crucial in determining such differences.[16] The school in the Basque Country thus reflects the peculiarities and tensions of a social dynamic associated with the place in which it is found.

BECAUSE the history the Basque school system parallels that of Basque nationalist demands, which are related to more general linguistic and cultural questions, one can see four distinct periods in the history of the Basque school.[17] During the first two periods, the few attempts to develop an education system linked to the local culture and/or to Euskara did not achieve any relevant levels, either quantitatively or qualitatively: Until the late nineteenth century, a search for Basque identity was the principal focus of nationalist efforts, while nationalism, as defined by its founder, Sabino Arana, was repressed until 1969 during the clandestine time of silence. In the era from 1970 to 1980, however, Basque nationalism underwent a redefinition, expanding into nontraditional nationalist sectors, and from 1981 to the present, it has been institutionalized and has enjoyed some the politico-administrative success. Thus here I will explore only the last two periods.

THE *IKASTOLA* PHENOMENON

During the third period, that of the redefintion and expansion of Basque nationalism under the protection of its powerful social framework, a number of educational projects flourished: literacy in Euskara, linguistic normalization and so on. Above all, there emerged a project (the necessity of creating a Basque education system) and a diagnosis (the historical decline of Basque as a consequence of the development of schooling in Spanish or French and the necessity to halt this retreat), that more or less justified the need to create a culturally and linguistically Basque system. Repressed and reduced to the family sphere, without any normalization or mechanisms to guarantee its continuity, Euskara—it was said—would disappear. Therefore it was necessary to think about its recovery and modernization but above all—it was concluded—its reproduction.

UNDER THE protection of this diagnosis, the education of infants became necessarily the most important object of social preoccupations of the time,[18] and the *ikastola* became the means to guarantee this reproduction. These *ikastolas*, undoubtedly a unique phenomenon, because they were created outside the official education system in semiclandestine conditions, often hidden in the basements of churches and promoted by ad hoc cooperatives formed by parents of the students, were much more than just educational spaces. They were, according to Jesús Arpal, "the operational synthesis undertaken practically by Basque culture at a moment

Basque-language schooling in towns
The Lauaxeta ikastola in Amorebieta, Bizkaia. Founded in 1977 and named after the poet and journalist Esteban Urkiaga ("Lauaxeta", 1905–37), this ikastola is a nonprofit, parent-owned cooperative school. Its Web site, available in English, Spanish, and Euskara, explains its educational goals: www.lauaxeta.net/
Photo: Iñaki Martínez de Albeniz.

---

of extreme crisis in the definition of this culture and its social meaning." Beyond this, they were born with the goal of being "the mythical redoubt ... of Basque identity against foreign imposition or the deterioration of its own customs,"[19]

FOLLOWING a modest beginning (three *ikastolas* with sixty students in 1960), in the 1960s there emerged the first hints of an institutionalization process with the development of a fairly important coordination policy between these centers involving common

Table 10

1982–83 SCHOOL YEAR

	Basque as a subject	Bilingual teaching	Teaching in Basque	No Basque taught
Araba	60.80%	8.27%	1.70%	29.20%
Bizkaia	60.30%	6.80%	7.47%	25.30%
Gipuzkoa	61.20%	11.20%	23.40%	4.14%

2002–3 SCHOOL YEAR

	Basque as a subject	Bilingual teaching	Teaching in Basque	No Basque taught
Araba	44.70%	27.20%	28.10%	0
Bizkaia	37.20%	20.20%	41.50%	1.10%
Gipuzkoa	14.20%	23.40%	62.40%	0

Students according to teaching model and historic territory

Between the 1982-83 and 2002-3 school years, matriculation in an educational model taught entirely in Basque increased throughout the Basque Autonomous Community. At the turn of the millennium, this model was strongest in Gipuzkoa, although the most pronounced growth (as a percentage change) had taken place in Araba.

Source: Author's calculation from EUSTAT (The Basque Institute of Statistics) data.

programs, pedagogical and linguistic training for teachers, and even use of the institutional cover of the Catholic Church. Without doubt, these were the first steps toward a Basque public education system, a successful beginning reflected by the spectacular growth in the numbers of matriculating students in the *ikastolas* in what is now the Basque Autonomous Community.

Thanks to this encouragement, during the late 1960s, the *ikastola* became a wide-ranging social practice with "an extraordinary meaning in the cultural codification of collective identity"[20] since one could argue that it covered socializing tasks in aspects far transcending the merely linguistic realm. In other words, the *ikastolas* didn't only *teach* in a language, but also served to *make* that same language, and with that the community defined by possessing it. For these reasons, the *ikastola* movement is unquestionably a unique educational phenomenon for its tremendous ideological complexity, tremendous organizational complexity, and tremendous ethnocultural complexity. It contained elements of Basque nationalist ideology and a high degree of Catholicism in its basic discourse, but also a certain progressive pedagogy. It was located at the center of a state/nonstate educational duality, a private system of education aspiring to become the nucleus of the Basque public education system and organized under the umbrella of an atypical institutionalization. And although it was aimed, in principle, at the Basque-speaking population and at maintaining Euskara, it has also reached out to the population that does not speak Basque with the goal of increasing the number of Basque speakers.

TODAY, the importance of the *ikastola* has declined because, with the institutionalization of the project and the beginning normalized activities in Euskara at other educational levels and in the public sector, the need for such centers has diminished. This in turn has pushed the *ikastola* movement into the private educational sphere or under the protection of the public administration. As a result, the resilient discourse of its founding years has lost plausibility amid the context of

Teaching in Basque
Children and teachers. Primary educational facilities in a Basque school.
Photo: Iñaki Martínez de Albeniz.

---

an increasingly normalized environment for Euskara in the same way that the original voluntary involvement of the parents and teachers has given way to control of education by the public administration and the growing professional nature of the educators. However, the history of the *ikastola* has in many ways shaped the educational map of the contemporary Basque Country.

THE BASQUE PUBLIC SCHOOL

FROM 1979 onward, approaches to teaching language were increasingly incorporated into the formal education system, thus removing from the *ikastola* movement its former task as the sole teaching institution in Basque.

In this way, the old aspiration of a Basque education system was realized in the form of the Law on Basque Public Schools and in the laws regulating the use of Euskara in the Basque education system, the Basic Law on Normalizing the Use of Euskara in 1982 and the Decree on Bilingual Linguistic Models in 1983. From these legal regulations, the Basque education system in both public and private high schools was structured according to three models: Model A, with all classes taught in Spanish, with Basque taught like any other subject; Model B, with all classes taught equally in both Spanish and Basque; or Model D, with all classes taught in Basque, with Spanish taught like any other subject.

A glance at the figures for students enrolled in each one of these models shows that teaching all classes in Basque has increased steadily at the same time as the other two approaches have declined. Teaching all classes in Spanish has declined progressively since the 1982–83 school year, while teaching all classes in Basque has increased during the same time, from 23.1 percent in 1982 to 41 percent in 2002–3. These changes have occurred throughout the three historic territories of the Basque Autonomous Community, but the change is especially notable in the case of Gipuzkoa, while Araba has undergone the least spectacular growth.

IN FACT, this growth in matriculation for Basque-language education explains the rising numbers of Basque speakers during the last few decades. Furthermore, it helps to explain why there are one in four Basque speakers over forty years of age, one in three of those aged between twenty and twenty-four, four out of ten among those fifteen to nineteen years old, and almost half of those aged fifteen or under.

THE SCHOOL AS A PLACE FOR NEGOTIATING AND CONSTRUCTING IDENTITY

As argued in a previous work by the authors of this text-book, the school is an "ecological cross space of cultures and generations."[21] The gathering of children in an educational center is one place where identities are (re)constructed and where stereotypes about other people and oneself are negotiated and take shape.

One might say, then, that the school reflects (but also produces) the divisions and distinctions of the social context in which it is found. This implies addressing the social distinctions that run through the Basque Country: Whether one is a Basque speaker or not, or was born in the Basque Country or not (and so on) are questions that also come into play in schools. For this reason, studying in one educational branch or another, studying in a public or a private school, and, most importantly, being a member of such an important symbolic center in the Basque Country as an *ikastola* constitute much more than just simple landmarks in a child's life: In fact, they make up a child's whole biography. As other sociological studies have shown,[22] attending a public school is associated with "low social status," with coming from an "immigrant family," and with being a "Spanish speaker," while studying in predominantly Euskara-based schools is considered an ethnic marker signaling a "Basque-speaking environment" and "Basque nationalism."

THE STEREOTYPES associated with students in each type of educational environment shape not only the image that they have of the other, but also their own sense of a shared identity and the way in which the school is experienced: "separation" or "parallel worlds" are expressions that define very well the imaginary context in which the school is experienced in moments when students from any one of the approaches to linguistic education interact among themselves in exclusive fashion, without any contact with students from other educational background. Thus, once more, the school comes to display the identity maps inherited from its environment; maps that are, at the same time, reproduced.

Lesson seven

LEARNING OBJECTIVES

1. To analyze the institution of the school as a socialization agent.
2. To understand the importance of the school in cultural reproduction.
3. To analyze the school as a cultural crossroads, especially in terms of interethnic negotiation and intergenerational consciousness.
4. To understand the importance of relations between the school and Basque nationalism, highlighting the special nature of *ikastolas*.

REQUIRED READING

Begoña Echeverria, "Basque Schooling: What Is It Good For?" PhD diss., University of California, San Diego, 2000 (Ann Arbor, Mich.: UMI Dissertation Services, 2001).

Paul Willis, *Learning to Labour: How Working Class Kids Get Working Class Jobs* (Farnborough: Saxon House, 1977).

SUGGESTED READING

Jesús Arpal, et al., *Educación y sociedad en el País Vasco* (Donostia: Txertoa, 1982).

Pierre Bourdieu, et al., *Reproduction in Education, Society and Culture* (London: Sage, 1990).

WRITTEN LESSON FOR SUBMISSION

1. Describe the special nature of the *ikastolas* and their importance in constructing Basque nationalist ideology during the 1960s. Bear in mind, when you come to form your argument, the effects that the consolidation of the Basque education system might have had on this ideology.
2. Critically examine the challenges facing the Basque school, taking account of the tendency toward multiculturalism in contemporary societies.

Iñaki Martínez de Albeniz

8 · The media as socializing agent

SUMMARY

Previous chapters examined the characteristics of several socialization agents in the Basque Country, both formal (the family and education) and informal (peer group relations and intersubjective life). To complete this picture, we will now look at the social institution that, most observers agree, today plays an increasingly significant role in the socialization processes of modern societies: the media.

A BASIC assumption of the sociology of modernization processes (as proposed by the likes of David Riesman, Talcott Parsons, Shmuel N. Eisenstadt, Edward A. Tiryakian, and others) is that in modern societies, the school and the media—that is, socialization agents that exhibit a significantly universal and more formal nature—concentrate socializing functions to the detriment of more specific and less formalized agents such as the family and peer-group relations. As in the modernization process itself, this practice of transferring the socializing function from some agencies to others is generally a long one.

In the Basque Country, however, this process took shape in particularly rapid fashion for political reasons. As mentioned above, to counteract the official-formal political order during the Franco regime (1939–75), Basque society created a complex parallel informal communication structure characterized by a very tight level of internal cohesion in which the family (above all), and noninstitutionally regulated intersubjective relations encompassed the basic socializing functions. Indeed, the deficit of political legitimacy during the Franco regime and the repression experienced by the Basque nationalist world prevented any other social and communication structures (although not economic ones) from modernizing. Thus, only after getting over the effect of the Franco years would Basque society finally start out on the road to modernizing its social structures.

The principal milestone in this transformation toward full modernity was the process of political institutionalization that started with the passing of the Statute of Gernika in 1979. As the Basque political system was institutionalized, the Basque Country underwent a spectacular transformation from the sociostructural point of view. In general, one might argue that, beginning with this institutionalization of a formal political sphere differentiated from that of more informal socialization agents such as the family or peer groups, the latter gradually lost the influence and importance as institutions of social and above all political reproduction they previously enjoyed during the Franco regime (See Section 2, Chapters 5 and 6), to the advantage of more formal agents, mainly in the education system and the media.

HERE I WILL address the role of the media. As previously stated, in terms of the development of its communications system, Basque society has not resembled modern information societies, or has done so only lately. This is because it was not until the disappearance of the Franco regime that, thanks to the support of a political institutional system (parties and other political institutions), a media system emerged to monopolize the functions of political representation and to replace as an agent of (mainly political) socialization the semiclandestine informal structure that had opposed the dictatorship. It was the Basque nationalist political parties that actually transformed the thick, informal, and clandestine social network that existed during the dictatorship into

Plurality of opinion
A range of daily newspapers available in the Basque Autonomous Community. This is one example of the day-to-day construction of Basque social reality, and the multiple newspapers on sale offer different social, political, and cultural perspectives on this reality.
Photo: Iñaki Martínez de Albeniz.

---

a structure of formal, open, and public communications designed to channel political debate. Basque society thus definitively joined the world of media-driven political communication.

IN THE LIGHT of this development, it is worth analyzing the Basque communications system from a twofold perspective: On the one hand, I will refer to the makeup of the system from the perspective of the groups that control the media through their form of ownership (public or private), ideological leaning, origin (regional/local or state), and location (the Basque Autonomous Community or the rest of the Spanish state). On the other, I will complement this analysis of the Basque

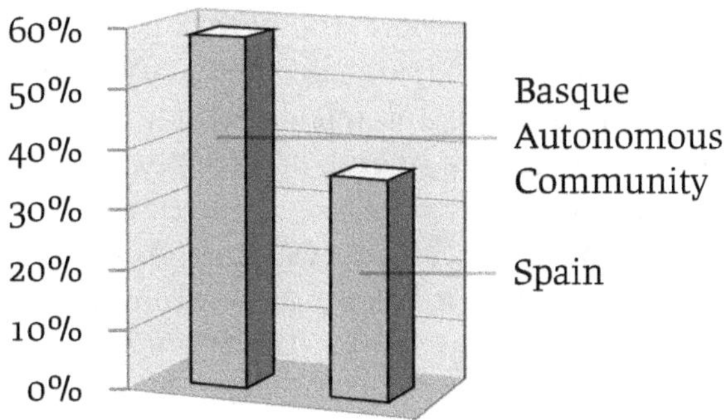

Table 11
Circulation and readership of the written press

	Basque Autonomous Community	Spain
Circulation Level of the Written Press	58.4%	36.4%

Circulation and readership of the written press
The Basque written press has a level of circulation and readership significantly higher than the written press in the Spanish state as a whole and even that of other countries, such as France. It approximates general European levels.
Source: General Survey of the Media.

communications system by an examination of media use by active audiences.

AN OVERVIEW OF THE BASQUE COMMUNICATIONS SYSTEM

The Basque communications system is characterized by its plural nature. Three subsystems can be highlighted. The first is composed of Spanish media delegations that have created regional terminals emanating from a political center (Madrid). Here, the newspapers *El País* and *El Mundo* are the principal print media, together with the larger Spanish radio and television stations. *El Mundo*'s editorial policies are liberal, and those of *El País* are social democratic.

The second, (and the subsystem of greater quantitative importance) is made up, as regards the written press, of organs associated with the conservative media tradition in the Basque Country that emerged in the late nineteenth century. These are media that have been present throughout the great historical debates between Basque and Spanish nationalism, as well as between conservative tendencies and strong left-wing working-class ideas. This subsystem is strongly linked to the Spanish political center in terms of its economic and ideological alliances. Today, the newspapers *El Correo* and *El Diario Vasco* are the main heirs to this tradition in the written press. Both belong to a communication group, Comecosa (also known as the Grupo Correo), that, is especially important in the Basque communications system. The journalistic business tradition of the Basque written press explains the dynamic nature of Comecosa as the leading regional press group in the Spanish state. The Comecosa group has a significant presence in all three historic Basque territories: *El Correo* in Araba and Bizkaia, and *El Diario Vasco* in Gipuzkoa.

THE THIRD subsystem is made up of local media that attempt to shape Basque public opinion. This subsystem is in the service of Basque nationalism, and its main argument is that the experiences and opinions that it represents were not reflected during the Franco years. These are, consequently, self-referential media. This subsystem is made up of the newspapers *Deia*, *Gara*, and

Broadcasting identity
The central studios of Euskal Irrati Telebista (EITB), the Basque public TV and radio service, in Durango, Bizkaia. EITB is a communication group that owns four television channels and five radio stations.
Photo: Iñaki Martínez de Albeniz.

Berria (the latter being the only daily in Basque), the public corporation Euskal Irrati Telebista (EITB, Basque Radio and Television), and various local media within specific areas of the Basque Country. *Deia* is ideologically close to the Basque Nationalist Party (PNV), while *Gara*, a pro-independence left-wing daily.

THE WRITTEN PRESS

The Basque written press has a level of circulation and readership close to the European average. Three Basque dailies are among the top ten circulating newspapers within the Spanish press as a whole. However, the non-Basque nationalist press remains important, despite Basque nationalism's electoral hegemony, and the Basque written press has been hampered by the difficulties of producing and maintaining a daily newspaper in Euskara.[23]

One of the most significant features of the Basque Country, in contrast to the rest of the Spanish state, is the high level of circulation and readership of the written press. The Basque Country has the second-highest circulation and readership after Navarre, a circulation and readership even larger than those in some countries with longer democratic histories, such as its neighbor France. This is a clear sign of the level of politicization in Basque society. In the 1960s, Basque nationalist political writing abandoned the clandestine realm in which it had been forced to hide during the Franco years, breaking out into the public sphere and thereby creating a Basque public-opinion system. In general, the figures, both for reading and circulation resemble standard European levels and leave Spanish figures somewhat behind.

DOMINANCE OF THE LOCAL PRESS

ANOTHER characteristic of the Basque press is the indisputable dominance of the regional or provincial press over its state counterpart. Local dailies account for 89.6 percent of sales, compared with 10.4 percent for newspapers published in Madrid.[24] There is, then, a clear preference for local media. In general, it is difficult for the Spanish written media to break into the Basque Country. This is due to the Basque Country's political and cultural (above all linguistic) specificity, together with the plural nature of its own media, which makes it unnecessary to turn to the state press in search of a

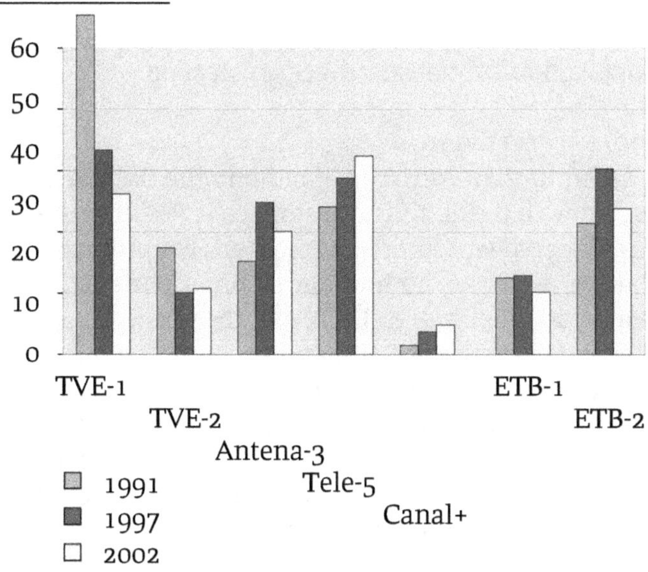

Table 12

		1991	1997	2002
State Channels	TVE-1	55.3	33.3	26.2
	TVE-2	17.4	10.1	10.8
	Antena-3	15.2	24.8	20.1
	Tele-5	24.1	28.8	32.4
	Canal +	1.5	3.7	4.9
Local Channels	ETB-1	12.5	12.9	10.2
	ETB-2	21.4	30.3	23.8

Evolution of television audience ratings
Television audience ratings in the Basque Autonomous Community at the end of the twentieth century demonstrate that no one single channel dominated, although the Spanish state channels (both public and private) continued to lead their Basque counterparts.
Source: CIES, A Study of the Autonomous Community Media. Columns add up to more than 100 percent because respondents watched more than one channel.

political position within the spectrum from the Basque nationalism to support for the Spanish state.[25]

RADIO AND TELEVISION

The defining characteristics of radio in the Basque Country begin with its significant audience levels. In addition, compared with other autonomous communities in the Spanish state, both public stations (the Basque Euskal Irrati Telebista, or EITB, and the Spanish Radio Nacional de España, or RNE) and smaller local ones are important. The existence of local free stations is a potent phenomenon. However, there is an imbalance, although less so than in the rest of the Spanish state, between the generally more influential radio stations operated from outside the autonomous community and local ones. The Basque Country also has its own public radio station (Radio Euskadi in Spanish, and Euskadi Irratia in Basque) covering different formats and the two languages.[26]

As regards television broadcasting in the Basque Autonomous Community, the most significant feature (as can be seen in Table 12) is the relative stability achieved in recent years.

No one channel is an absolute leader. Throughout the 1990s, the ratings for TVE-1, the public channel with the biggest audience and a channel that previously held a monopoly, declined a little, but maintained an average share of over 25 percent, while TVE-2 maintained a stable audience, close to 10 percent of the market. The general private channels, Antena-3 and Tele-5, recently have maintained shares of around 20 percent. One should also note that a major shareholder in Tele-5 is Comecosa.

ETB-1 and ETB-2 belong to the autonomous public group EITB. These two channels have no competition within the local and regional sphere, since the rest of the channels are broadcast from outside the Basque Autonomous Community or at most just have correspondents there. Furthermore, ETB-1 monopolizes television broadcasting in Euskara. These two channels have grown considerably in recent years and now represent strong competition for the larger state channels, managing to control nearly a fourth of the overall Basque television market.

Despite the growth of the EITB group's two channels, only a small part of the political information consumed in the Basque Country originates in Basque broadcasting circles: approximately one fourth, at the best of times, of the total information received. In sum, although EITB has achieved more and more diffusion, the state media still dominate in both radio and television.

MEDIA USE IN THE BASQUE COUNTRY

In general, audiovisual media are consumed for entertainment. As regards the dissemination of information, the audiovisual media are significantly complemented by the print media, more than in the rest of the Spanish state. Moreover, according to audience figures, three-quarters of the Basque population consume audiovisual media with a low degree of decentralization. One exception, however, is worth noting: When it comes to getting news information, the Basque audience tends toward local media.

USING THIS data, experts typically refer to a complex and, to some extent, schizoid or two-faced public opinion. Basque public opinion swings between political behavior and consumption of televised entertainment, between reading local newspapers and also reading those (*El Correo* and *El Diario Vasco*) that encompass a vision of Spanish unity, between a social mobilization practically monopolized by left-wing Basque national-

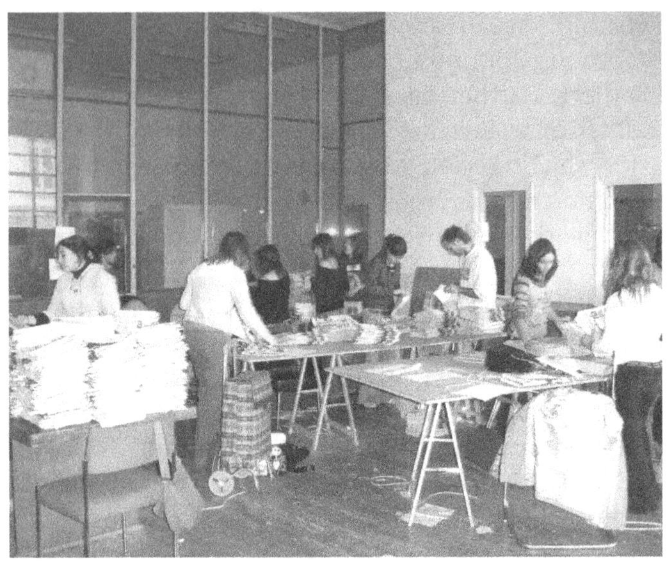

Popular press initiatives
The local press phenomenon in the Basque Country. Young volunteers help to distribute Goienkaria, a weekly newspaper in the High Deba region of Gipuzkoa. *Photo: Iñaki Martínez de Albeniz.*

---

ism during the last twenty years (and only really ever challenged by pacifist movements in the 1990s) and the consumption of media characterized by an adherence to state-level political parties.

THE BASQUE COMMUNICATIONS SYSTEM: BETWEEN THE LOCAL AND THE GLOBAL

The Basque communications system also demonstrates its greatest flexibility and vitality in the realm of what might be termed the unconventional media. Here, the heterogeneity and wealth of communication strategies in the Basque Country, together with the inevitable tensions produced in this environment between the local and the expanding global sectors, can be clearly seen. Two examples highlight these tensions: the potent phenomenon of local magazines and, as an example of the still-developing but increasing expansion of the Basque media toward the Internet, the Web site of Eusko News and Media, euskonews.com.

LOCAL MAGAZINES

The majority of local media in the Basque Autonomous Community grew as a result of a social demand for publications in Euskara. These are typically self-published weekly or biweekly magazines that have a small editorial team with two or three full-time journalists, supported by a number of volunteers. The magazines themselves are usually distributed free of charge to the homes of a given town or area. Their total print run numbers around four million annually, and they cover a demand that no other medium addresses. Most of these magazines are financed from mixed sources: They both receive public funding and survive economically by selling advertising.

THE LEVEL of institutionalization that such local magazines have acquired was reflected by the foundation in 1997 of a federation of associations that brings together all local magazines in the Basque Country. Its name is Topagunea (Meeting Place), and it has sixty-one members: three in Araba, thirty-one in Gipuzkoa, and twenty-five in Bizkaia. As one can see, there is a big difference between the three historic territories. This is because 80 percent of Basque speakers live in either Gipuzkoa or Bizkaia.

In the words of José Mari Muxika, the coordinator of Topagunea, "the growth of Basque-language magazines emerged out of associations that wanted to defend Basque. The initiative came out of civil society, as in many other cases and initiatives. In the audiovisual media, EITB covers the task of normalizing Basque use. However, in the written press sector, this is done by local magazines." Apart from managing and promoting local magazines, this federation offers general services and cultural innovation and creation, attends to the needs of children and young people, and helps promote Basque.

OF ALL THE initiatives associated with Topagunea, without any doubt the case of the ARKO (Arrasateko Komunikabideak) cooperative stands out. It began as a magazine offering local information, but with the passage of time, ARKO has become a full-blown multimedia communications group. The cooperative, located in the town of Mondragón (Gipuzkoa) and its surrounding area—where such cooperative initiatives have a long tradition, to the point of being an international point of reference—forms part of the Goiena Company. Goiena publishes a daily newspaper in the area, *Goienkaria*, as well as having a local radio station and television channel. ARKO is an obvious reference point for the future development of such local activities, as regards both territorial expansion and the diversification of communication channels. However, despite its expansion and diversification, ARKO did not as of spring 2005 have a Web site. This is but one example of the scant presence of Basque media on the Internet.

BASQUE MEDIA ON THE INTERNET

Internet use in the Basque Country is not comparable with Internet use in other European countries, and even less so with that in the United States. It is estimated that 2.7 percent of the Basque population uses the Internet, while in countries such as Sweden or Germany, this figure rises to 6 percent and 8 percent, respectively.

No Basque Web site appears among those most visited in the Spanish state. Similarly, among the media consulted at that level, large Basque print dailies such as *El Correo* and *El Diario Vasco* do not appear on the Web at all. However, the reverse is true of Spanish newspapers: Despite having lower sales figures for their paper editions, newspapers such as *El País*, *ABC*, and *El Mundo*, together with certain search engines such as Yahoo and Microsoft, are the most visited Web sites among Basque Internet users.

HOWEVER, in spite of the scarce presence of Basque media on the Internet, new initiatives have emerged, such as that of the Web site Euskonews and Media (www.euskonews.com) by Eusko Ikaskuntza (the Basque Studies Society). Here, the section KOSMOpolita—aimed at diffusing through the Internet "the current and historical Basque presence throughout the world" by means of articles written by "Basques living on the five continents"—especially stands out (see Section 3, Chapter 18).

Lesson eight

LEARNING OBJECTIVES

1. To understand in detail the growing importance of the media at the expense of other agents such as the family and, to a lesser extent, peer groups and schools, in socialization processes.
2. To identify the main features of the Basque communications system's emergence and the share, in terms of influencing public opinion, enjoyed by both local and state media.

---

3. To analyze the Basque public's use of the media and why they do so (whether to get information, be entertained, and so on).
4. To evaluate the media at a global level and its presence on the Internet.

REQUIRED READING

Josu Amezaga, Edorta Arana, Ander Iturriotz, and Rosa María Martín, "Public Opinion, Published Opinion and the Opinion of the Public: Media Influence in Basque Politics," *Uztaro* 22 (1987): 41–57. English version at http://ibs.lgu.ac.uk/forum/politx.htm.

Patxi Azpillaga, "The Structure of the Mass Media," paper delivered at the First International Symposium on Basque Cultural Studies, London Guildhall University, 2000; http://ibs.lgu.ac.uk/sympo/page4.html.

SUGGESTED READING

Mikel Arriaga, Andrés Davila, and J. L. Pérez Soengas. "Difusión de los diarios en Euskalherria desde la transición política: De lo ordinal a lo cardinal," *ZER* 10 (2001); http://www.ehu.es/zer/zer10/arriaga.html.

Ramón Zallo, ed., *Industrias y políticas culturales en España y País Vasco* (Bilbao: Servicio Editorial de la Universidad del País Vasco, 1995).

WRITTEN LESSON FOR SUBMISSION

1. Outline the basic features of the Basque communications system.
2. Critically assess the dominance of the local press and point out the consequences of this for politics and the shaping of Basque public opinion.

Alfonso Pérez-Agote

9 · Religion and collective identity

SUMMAry

This chapter addresses the role of the Catholic Church in maintaining the cultural foundations of Basque nationalism, and especially Euskara, through the production and reproduction of literature and, later, during the Franco years, as a protector of popular organizations out of which important associative links were established that nourished the Basque nationalist consciousness. Within this distinctive politico-religious framework, the chapter will also explore the equally important secularization process in a society that attained a significant level of industrialization.

THE CATHOLIC Church and religious tradition in the Basque Country have played a crucial role in the reproduction of Basque nationalism. The church was especially important in preserving Euskara, particularly between the seventeenth and nineteenth centuries, a period in which, in the context of social change, the church—traditional society's most important institution—developed strategies for its survival.

THE CLERGY AND LITERATURE IN BASQUE

According to Luis Michelena, "the real Basque mystery" is "the preservation, not the origin, of the language." Michelena attributed to the Catholic Church and its clergymen an important role in helping the Basque language, principally from the seventeenth century onward. He continues:

> In addition to documents of tremendous value to the history of the language, we owe them, among many verses, a model of literary prose that still today main-

> tains its original inspirational force. ... On this side of the border [the Spanish Basque Country], this model greatly influenced eighteenth- and early nineteenth-century authors, principally from Gipuzkoa and Bizkaia. ... What should be pointed out is that at that time, a form of religion (dogma, morality, rites, discipline) took root that subsequently came to be known through the widespread identification of the secular and regular clergy with the people. This identification was particularly evident in language issues, where the criteria of religious content and preaching constituted for a long time almost the only prose guide.[27]

HOWEVER, Ibon Sarasola contends that by the nineteenth century, an important development in secular Basque-language literature had taken place, and lay institutions, training a new intellectual elite, were also growing in importance. According to Sarasola,

> For the first time in history, the clergy in the Basque Country felt seriously threatened. Seeing that the ruling classes were increasingly moving away from its influence, and with a view to improving its ties to the regular people, the uncivilized people who spoke Basque and were uncivilized [precisely] because they spoke it, it found a change of tactics necessary. From then on, Basque was not just a language like any other, but a defensive wall to be raised against new ideas. The Basque language thus became, for the Basque clergy, a language to protect in order to maintain its retrograde ideas.[28]

This would explain the general adherence of the Basque clergy to Carlism—a conservative political ideology created in the nineteenth century to defend traditional society against the rising force of liberalism—and their

Religion and politics
The San Antón Church, Bilbao, Bizkaia. Here, the first mass in Euskara was celebrated during the Franco regime, and it served as an important shelter of Basque nationalism at that time.
Photo: Iñaki Martínez de Albeniz.

later support, in Gipuzkoa and Bizkaia, at least, for Basque nationalism prior to the outbreak of the Spanish Civil War in 1936.

ONE MIGHT deduce, from the thoughts of these two eminent scholars of the Basque language and its history, two relationships: first, the relationship of religion and the clergy with the language, as indicated by the importance of religious literature and the general participation of the clergy in literary production from the sixteenth century through the nineteenth century (see Table 13), and second, the relationship of the clergy

Table 13

		Total Production	Nonreligious Production
16th C	2nd Half	1	1
17th C	1st Half	6	0
	2nd Half	6	1
18th C	1st Half	5	1
	2nd Half	24	1
19th C	1st Half	26	1
	2nd Half	33	4

Production of books in Basque

Literary production in Basque between the sixteenth and nineteenth centuries was clearly linked to the diffusion of religious material.

Source: Ibon Sarasola, Historia social de la literatura vasca *(Madrid: Akal, 1976), 183.*

Table 14

Social Class	France	Basque Country
Nobility	28%	0%
Clergy	6%	90%
Third Estate	66%	10%

Basque and French writers according to social stratum, 1500–1800

Compared with France, literary production in the Basque Country between the sixteenth and eighteenth centuries was dominated by the clergy, and the Basque nobility took no active part in writing in Euskara.

Source: "The French Book Trade in the Ancient Regime," cited in Ibon Sarasola, Historia social de la literatura vasca *(Madrid: Akal, 1976), 53.*

Table 15

	1934–1935	1972–1973
Total Books Published	19	101
Essay and Social Sciences	5.80%	36.60%
Religion	20%	3%

Basque-language publications (first editions, reprints, and translations), by subject

Comparing data from the mid-1930s and the early 1970s, one can see that, as a subject for literary production in Basque, religion declined significantly in the intervening period.

Source: Ibon Sarasola, Historia social de la literatura vasca *(Madrid: Akal, 1976), 8–19.*

with the people, which in part overlapped with the first connection. Yet one should also emphasize that Michelena's argument is mainly valid (in his opinion, too) for Bizkaia and Gipuzkoa, the historic territories where Basque nationalism later became important and where most Basque speakers, both before and after the Spanish Civil War (1936–39), were found. Consequently, it would appear that the two relationships highlighted by Michelena constitute a sound explanatory hypothesis of the later close relationship between religion and the clergy and Basque nationalism and the Basque language.

LOOKING at the following tables, certain interesting conclusions emerge. First, one should highlight the important growth of Basque-language literature and authors. Second, if one compares the data relative to 1934–35 with that of 1972–73, one sees that a major secularization process took place in both the literature itself and the religious affiliations of the authors.

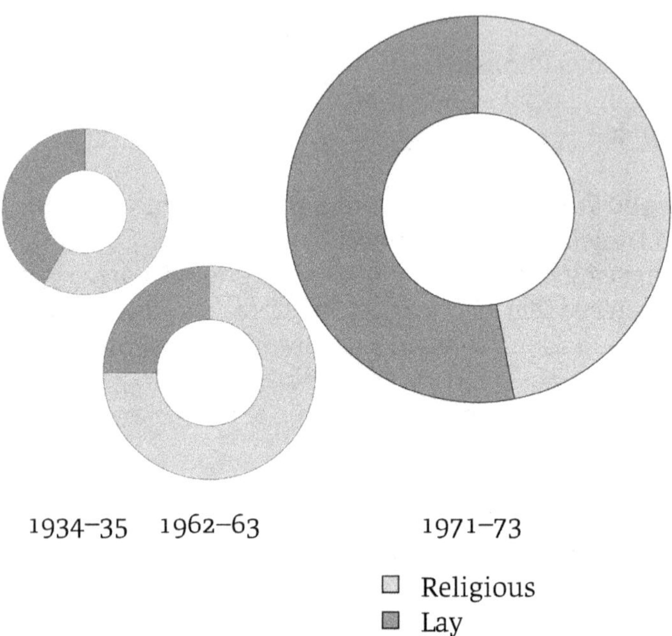

Table 16

	1934–1935	1962–1963	1971–1973
Total	12	20	65
Lay	41.60%	25%	53.10%
Religious	58.40%	75%	46.90%

Basque-Language authors by religious affiliation
Although the religious affiliation of Basque-language authors actually increased between the 1930s and the 1960s as writers took refuge in the church, subsequently a secularization process took place among these same authors between the early 1960s and the early 1970s. *Source: Ibon Sarasola,* Historia social de la literature vasca *(Madrid: Akal, 1976), 20.*

However, the process is not linear. This was because the repression of the Basque language and culture after the Spanish Civil War ended in 1939 forced both sets of authors once more to take refuge in the church.

THE CATHOLIC CHURCH AND POLITICS DURING THE FRANCO YEARS

THE CHURCH was a potential refuge for all those opposed to or critical of the Franco regime, because its organizational nature was closely tied to the lower classes and it possessed locations throughout Spain in a society where the right of free assembly was strictly

Table 17

	Primary education 1968–69	**Secondary education 1967–68**	**Higher education 1974–75**
1 Araba	18.1%	55.7%	0%
2 Gipuzkoa	12.1%	46.3%	65.8%
3 Bizkaia	24.3%	41.6%	30.8%
4 Navarre	28.1%	48.1%	100.0%
1+2+3+4	21.5%	45.4%	49.0%
Spain	14.7%	32.2%	3.7%

Students in religious schools as a percentage of the total students in the same grade, by province
During the final years of the Franco regime, while the church was an important source of education in Spain as a whole, it remained even more important in the Basque Country, accounting for nearly half of all students in both secondary and higher education.
Source: Luis C. Núñez, La sociedad vasca actual *(San Sebastián: Txertoa, 1977), 61.*

From religiosity and patrimony
Churches in the Basque Country have been transformed from influential centers shaping social life into places of architectural and aesthetic interest.
Photo: Iñaki Martínez de Albeniz.

prohibited. Similarly, the church in the Basque Country, which was very closely tied to the Basque nationalist cause, offered a natural refuge for both the Basque language and culture.[29] This would lead to a great deal of tension at the heart of the church itself between the hierarchy, strongly associated with the political power center during the Franco regime, and the simple clergy, who, being more in touch with grass-roots social reality, swiftly changed both their social ideas and their activities as a result of the upheaval produced by industrialization, immigration, and political repression at that time.

Table 18

Place	(a) 1960	(a) 1975	(b) 1990
BAC + Navarre	27%	18%	15%
Spain	100%	100%	100%

Bishops born in the Basque Autonomous Community (BAC) and Navarre

In 1960, a quarter of all bishops in Spain came from the BAC and Navarre. However, by 1990, this proportion had fallen to one-sixth, demonstrating the importance of the secularization process that took place in the intervening years.

Source: (a) Luis C. Núñez, La sociedad vasca actual *(San Sebastián: Txertoa, 1977), 56, (b)* Anuario de la Iglesia en España *(1990), 213.*

Table 19

	1960	1975
BAC + Navarre	1.8%	1.1%
Spain	0.8%	0.7%

Priests per thousand inhabitants

While the number of priests per thousand inhabitants in the BAC and Navarre remained above the average level for Spain as a whole in the period from 1960 to 1975, the decline in Basques joining the priesthood during the same period was more marked than at the state level.

Source: Luis C. Núñez, La sociedad vasca actual *(San Sebastián: Txertoa, 1977), 82.*

Table 20

		BAC + Navarre	Spain
(a) 1960	No.	754	8,021
	%	9.40%	100%
(a) 1968	No.	855	6,995
	%	12.20%	100%
(a) 1975	No.	140	2,371
	%	5.90%	100%
(b) 1990	No.	89	1,999
	%	4.40%	100%

Evolution of the number and proportion of higher seminarians

During the 1960s, the number of higher seminarians in the BAC and Navarre actually grew, in contrast to the statistics for Spain as a whole, demonstrating the continued importance of seminaries as both religious and educational centers at this time. Thereafter, however, during the 1970s and 1980s, the number of people attending seminary in the BAC and Navarre declined more dramatically than the Spanish average.

Source: (a) Luis C. Núñez, La sociedad vasca actual *(San Sebastián: Txertoa, 1977), 86, (b)* Anuario de la Iglesia en España, *129–75.*

ADDITIONALLY, during the Franco era, the church also played an important role in two basic aspects of the reproduction, extension, and strengthening of Basque nationalist consciousness that took place at that time. The Church played a role in the education system, in particular, via the seminaries and novitiates of different religious orders, whose function was to reproduce the clergy. In part, one might argue that

After religion, leisure
The old seminary in Derio, Bizkaia, today converted into a hotel. A dramatic fall in the number of seminarians has made it necessary to restructure these grand buildings into viable contemporary enterprises. The seventy-six room Hotel Andrea now serves visitors to Bilbao and the neighboring Zamudio Technology Park.
Photo: Iñaki Martínez de Albeniz.

during the 1950s and 1960s, such centers were the only possible places where written Basque was able to survive and to develop. In this sense, the collaboration of seminary and novitiate students (for example, Franciscans, Benedictines, Sacramentines, Jesuits, Carmelites, and Passionists) in Basque-language magazines was especially important. Such collaboration also encouraged the institutionalization of meetings between different authors, meetings in which they even began to come to some agreement about the grammatical rules of the Basque language. This was especially important, because Euskara had been socially maintained through mainly oral means, and during the 1950s and 1960s, these religious centers offered the only possibility of learning to read and write in Euskara for Basque speakers.[30]

THESE FACTS do not contradict the preceding statements about the secularization of Basque literature. As previously mentioned, between 1971 and 1973, for the first time in history, the number of Basque-language lay writers 53.1 percent of the total) outnumbered their religious counterparts, yet of these, 20.6 percent had attended a seminary or novitiate, only to become secular later.[31] The social importance implied by this internment of written Basque did not end in the linguistic or

Table 21

		Spain	BAC + Navarre
1955	No.	0	106
	%	0%	0%
1963	No.	616	75
	%	100%	12.10%
1975	No.	321	18
	%	100%	5.60%

Number and proportion of priests' ordinations
Both the number and proportion (as a percentage of the Spanish total) of priests' ordinations declined steadily between the mid-1950s and the mid-1970s in the BAC and Navarre.
Source: Luis C. Núñez, La sociedad vasca actual *(San Sebastián: Txertoa, 1977), 90.*

literate realm. Rather, it came accompanied by the fact that these centers also constituted an authentic social means of developing the Basque nationalist consciousness. If one takes into account the fact that, after the end of the Spanish Civil War in 1939 (and above all in rural areas), the only possibility of continuing one's standard level or higher education for people from families with low or middle incomes was offered by schools attached to novitiates or by the novitiates and seminaries them-

Table 22

	% of population older than seven
Andalusia	22.4%
Aragon	61.3%
Balearic Islands	58.3%
Canary Islands	22.4%
New Castile	17.6%
Old Castile and León	65.3%
Catalonia	21.7%
BAC + Navarre	71.3%
Extremadura	26.7%
Galicia and Asturias	40.8%
Valencia and Murcia	30.2%
Spain	34.6%

Sunday mass attendance in Spain, 1972
According to the 1972 statistics for Mass attendance, the BAC and Navarre remained clearly the most religious region in Spain, with a percentage double that of the Spanish national average.
Source: Luis Núñez, La sociedad vasca actual *(San Sebastián: Txertoa, 1977), 68.*

selves, it is easy to understand why these religious centers and seminaries were so important in terms of reproducing the nationalist consciousness.

THIS SAID, however, one must still recognize the more general importance of the church in education, which was significant in Spain as a whole, but was still more central in the Basque Country, as one sees from the figures in Table 17.

Table 23

Definition	**Spain**	**BAC**
Practicing Catholic	42%	43%
Nonpracticing Catholic	41%	38%
Christian, but not Catholic	3%	4%
Another religion	1%	1%
Believer, but without belonging to any religion	4%	3%
Agnostic	3%	3%
Nonbeliever	5%	7%
No Answer	1%	1%

Religious self-definition as a percentage of the total population in Spain and the Basque Autonomous Community, 1987

By the late 1980s, the religious identification of inhabitants in the Basque Autonomous Community closely resembled Spanish averages.

Source: Alfonso Pérez-Agote, *Los lugares sociales de la religión: La secularización de la vida en el País Vasco* (Madrid: Centro de Investigaciones Sociológicas, 1990), 37.

The church also developed an important role in what has been termed the associative world. The church's relative political immunity, together with its network of various locations, frequently allowed it to serve as a front for the numerous clandestine activities of both the working-class and Basque nationalist movements. Yet the church did not only lend its locations for these activities, but often also served as an inspirational force, an instigator and maintainer of much of the associative world, especially at the youth level. During the Franco period, a number of these associations were linked in different ways to their parishes, priests, and so on. This associative world proved to be important as a mechanism for producing and reproducing an ever-radicalizing Basque nationalist consciousness, both political and social.

THE INCREASING tension with both the church hierarchy and the main political authorities during the Franco era that resulted from this social and political activity on the part of the clergy led to the publication of a series of documents throughout the period in which the clergy time and time again denounced both the religious and political hierarchies. In the Basque Country, this conflict gradually ceased to be posed in terms of political questions relating to ethnic differences and began to focus on ethnic and social problems with, as a backdrop, an attempt to deny legitimacy to state violence while legitimizing (in terms of necessity) the antistate variety.[32]

THE SECULARIZATION PROCESS IN THE BASQUE COUNTRY

The Basque Country has been until relatively recently a very religious area, compared with average Spanish levels of faith. This high degree of religiosity was maintained, of course, in spite of a relatively high level of

After religion, rock
The old La Merced church, Bilbao, Bizkaia, now a municipal concert hall, Bilborock. This seventeenth-century building is now home to three floors, with a capacity for 300 (seated) or 500 (standing). Where once people attended a daily or weekly Mass, they now flock to weekly concerts. Information in English at: www.bilbao.net/bilborock/
Photo: Iñaki Martínez de Albeniz.

---

industrialization and development, again compared with Spanish averages. However, today, levels of religious belief in the Basque Country approximate more closely the Spanish average, because in the 1970s, the Basque Country underwent a more intense secularization process than Spanish society as a whole.

Table 24

	Spain	BAC
Never	27%	30%
Several Times a Day	30%	23%
Occasionally throughout the Year	11%	12%
Almost every Sunday	14%	16%
Every Sunday and on Holidays	17%	19%

Frequency of mass attendance as a percentage of the total population in Spain and the Basque Autonomous Community, 1987

Source: Alfonso Pérez-Agote, Los lugares sociales de la religión: La secularización de la vida en el País Vasco *(Madrid: Centro de Investigaciones Sociológicas, 1990), 38.*

THERE ARE a number of ways to gauge the fact that, until recently, this traditional form of religious faith drawn towards the Church in the Basque Country was appreciably higher than the Spanish average.[33] In Table 18, for example, one can see the proportion of bishops born in the Basque Country. In 1960, more than one in four Spanish bishops were Basque, although the Basque population represented only 5 percent of the Spanish total at that time. Yet one can also see that this proportion gradually declined over time. Similarly, at that time, the number of churches per thousand inhabitants in the Basque Country was 2.3 percent, while the Spanish average was 1.4 percent.[34] Table 19 demonstrates the similarity of statistics regarding the number of priests per thousand inhabitants, while in Table 20 one can observe how in 1960, higher seminarians from the Basque Country represented 9.4 percent of the Spanish total, a proportion that continued to rise until 1968, when it reached 12.2 percent. This increase was due to the fact that while in the rest of Spain the number of higher seminarians decreased, between 1960 and 1968 in the Basque Country, it actually rose. Later, around 1970, the fall in both the numbers and the proportions became quite striking. This would seem to indicate that religious belief oriented toward the church was still very strong in the 1960s, although one should add (as previously explained) that in both the 1950s and 1960s, seminaries offered important educational opportunities. This would support the fact that while the number of higher seminarians grew during the 1960s, that was not the case (as can be seen from Table 21) with the number of priests' ordinations.[35]

INFORMATION on religious practice itself is scarce. According to most experts, Rogelio Duocastella was the first observer to address this issue seriously when in 1967 he drew up the first map of religious practice in Spain. He speaks of "an extremely intense and very homogeneous religious experience in the Basque-Navarrese region, fractured [only] by the industrial area of Bilbao."[36] He calculates attendance at Mass for the region at between 75 and 100 percent, falling to 53.6 percent in the Bilbao "fracture," attributing this lower percentage to high immigration into that area from other less-practicing regions in the south of Spain.[37] In Table 22, also based on Duocastella's data and cited by Núñez, in *Opresión y defensa en Euskera*, one can see how in 1972 the proportion of Sunday worshippers was still much higher than the Spanish average. Indeed, at the time, there was greater attendance at Mass than in any other region of Spain. Although there are also data for 1987, they are not as consistent as those for 1972. One can, however, still deduce that religious faith and practice in the Basque Autonomous Community was very similar to the Spanish average at that time. Table 23 shows how religious self-definition is similar in both the BAC and Spain as a whole, while Table 24 demonstrates that religious practice in the BAC is somewhat lower than the Spanish average. This would imply that between 1972 and 1987, a significant process of secularization took place, more than the average rate in Spain.

Lesson nine

LEARNING OBJECTIVES

1. To understand the importance of the Catholic Church in preserving the Basque language, especially through literary production.
2. To analyze the effect of the Catholic Church on reproducing Basque nationalist consciousness.
3. To understand some indicative factors of the Basque secularization process.
4. To link this secularization process to industrial modernization in the Basque Country.

REQUIRED READING

Alfonso Pérez-Agote, "The Role of Religion in the Definition of a Symbolic Conflict: Religion and the Basque Problem." *Social Compass* 33, no. 4 (1986): 419–35.

Thomas Luckmann, *The Invisible Religion* (London: Macmillan, 1967).

SUGGESTED READING

Luis C. Núñez, *Opresión y defensa en Euskera* (San Sebastián: Txertoa, 1977).

Luis C. Núñez, *La sociedad vasca actual* (San Sebastián: Txertoa, 1977).

WRITTEN LESSON FOR SUBMISSION

1. Critically examine the relationship between political modernization and secularization in the Basque Country.
2. In your opinion, why might religious belief be higher in rural areas than in urban ones?

Benjamín Tejerina

10 · Language and collective identity

SUMMARY

This chapter studies changes in Basque identity through an examination of the articulations to which Euskara has been historically subjected. Euskara is a clear example of how definitions of Basque identity have transformed from an emphasis on ethnic or biological elements to framing Basque difference in purely socio-cultural terms: in other words, from the racialization of Euskara, or its conversion into a distinctive sign of a certain race, to its ethnicization, or definition as the cultural value of a community, and politicization, or use as a banner signifying certain political leanings.

THE DEFINITIONS that social actors make of their collective identity usually differ from one historical era to another and may even vary according to the time and place in which they find themselves. However, a consideration of the historical development of these definitions reveals that such change has mostly been slow, alternating between fairly stable moments (marked by the extension of a certain definition of group identity) and other times when such ideas have been subject to change and redefinition. These changes are closely linked to socio-structural transformation processes that run through society as a whole and to those people or social groups that shape and carry out these specific definitions.

The trajectory of the definitions of collective identity that emerged out of Basque nationalist sectors during the last century developed from an original emphasis on ethnic and biological elements to one resting on socio-cultural aspects. Within this process, the Basque language, already present among those initial definitions (although occupying a secondary position), gradually acquired more and more importance until eventually it became the most important critical element on which social actors based the differential nature of Basque national identity.

THE RECENT HISTORICAL DEVELOPMENT OF THE BASQUE LANGUAGE

Euskara is a language that has lost importance historically due to the several recent sociohistorical factors. These include the effects of an increasingly urbanizing society from the mid-eighteenth century onward, the ambivalence of the church, and the role of both inward and outward migration. Euskara had been repressed and marginalized in the educational system and was disparaged among well-to-do and educated people. It was also marginalized and overlooked by public institutions.

THE INDUSTRIALIZATION process, beginning in the second half of the nineteenth century and developing (at varying rates) through to the 1970s was especially important. The demographic, urban, and socioeconomic changes that accompanied the modernization process would also have a major influence on linguistic practice among Basques (see Section 1, Chapters 1 and 3).

COLLECTIVE IDENTITY AND LINGUISTIC CONSCIOUSNESS

Attempts to promote and to defend the Basque language have a long history in the Basque Country. Prior to the eighteenth century, there were numerous examples of a linguistic consciousness and of more or less successful attempts to stimulate Euskara's development and extension. However, in the nineteenth century, this linguistic consciousness acquired a new dimension by teaming

Religion as a sanctuary of Euskara
The Arantzazu Sanctuary, Gipuzkoa. The first grammar of standard or unified Euskara was drawn up in the sanctuary in the 1960s, demonstrating the important role the church has played in fomenting the Basque language. *Photo: Iñaki Martínez de Albeniz.*

---

up with nationalist currents of thought sweeping across Europe at the time.

AS A RESULT, the situation of Euskara attracted the interest of a group of intellectuals led by Arturo Campión who, from 1876 onward, began to develop a project of cultural recovery, first in Navarre and later throughout the whole Basque region. He identified the language as the most significant factor in the Basque collective consciousness and linked the latter's destiny to the fluctuating fortunes of the former.

The most significant feature about Campión was that he did not limit himself to merely denouncing the decline of the language, but actually analyzed this fall, noting each and every factor that had combined to produce the situation: the disdain for Euskara among the upper classes, its absence in the educational system and repression by teachers, the increasing ease of communications facilitating greater population movement, the impoverishment of the language and its failure to adapt to modern life, the multiple dialects, subdialects, and varieties, and the low esteem of the language among the lower classes.

THE RACIALIZATION OF EUSKARA

The social transformations that took place in Bizkaia during the last third of the nineteenth century altered social reality and traditional lifestyles there in ways that differed from what prevailed in the rest of the Basque Country. In the 1890s, within this context of tremendous social change, Sabino Arana tried to project a new political vision of Basque identity by defining it in national terms.

FOR ARANA, Basque nationality rested on five elements: race, language, government and laws (the foral heritage, as discussed in Section 1, Chapter 2), character and customs, and historic personality. Each element had its own specific importance, with the five aspects thereby making a hierarchy.

The fundamental, indisputable element of Basque nationality for Arana was race. From the point of view of ethnic characteristics, he claimed, Basques constitute a race different from the rest, with both their history and their language demonstrating the dynamic and creative nature of the Basque national character. Basques' habits, features, and customs were seen to be determined by their race. Independently of individual will, race was supposed to be the differential element that made the Basque nation distinctive.

THE WAY TO maintain this racial difference, Arana claimed, was to preserve its special linguistic nature, and in this sense, the language was seen as at the same time both an integrating mechanism of social cohesion and one of ethnic differentiation. In effect, for Arana, what allowed one to speak of the persistence through time of the Basque people was their occupation of the same territory by a group of racially distinct individuals who used the same communicative code: Euskara. From these two factors, the unique government and laws, character and customs, and historic personality of the Basques were said to follow, thereby forming Arana's aforementioned hierarchy of essential characteristics defining Basque identity; a hierarchy rooted in the most important element, race, that in turn imparted Basques with their remaining key features: language, laws, customs, and, finally, historic personality.

THE ETHNICIZATION OF EUSKARA: THE CULTURAL RENAISSANCE

Sabino Arana's premature death in 1903 did not result in the demise of Basque nationalist ideology. Quite the contrary, in fact, for the subsequent decades saw the consolidation and expansion of his ideas. Together with the development of the Basque Nationalist Party (PNV), a number of organizations were formed that brought widely different social sectors into the nationalist movement. Ultimately, these would make up an extremely internally dynamic social framework or "microsociety" that sustained Basque nationalist mobilization. Within this process of expansion the contribution of Father José Ariztimuño (also known as "Aitzol") especially stood out.

He reworked the role the language played for Basque nationalists and proposed the necessary practical tasks for making such a reshaped role possible.

For Ariztimuño the value of the language, more than its intrinsic worth as a means of communication or as an agent to transmit scientific knowledge, rested on its capacity to shape a collective mentality. He saw language as a unifying link, a nucleus, a soul, and a central value in the collective consciousness of any ethnic group, beyond being a mere differentiating factor of race. Thus, he saw two differentiated collective souls in the Basque Country, each of which possessed a different language. Ariztimuño frequently used the expression "language struggle," and this demonstrated (as regarded the Basque Country) the agonizing situation into which the autochthonous tongue had fallen. Threatened by Spanish (which dominated the education system), the situation thus called for every effort to recover Basque.

THE POLITICIZATION OF EUSKARA

As a consequence of Basque nationalism's defeat in the Spanish Civil War, the Franco regime (1939–75) introduced a widespread policy of systematically repressing all Basque nationalist symbols. Within this general policy, the public spheres of the school and the streets were particularly singled out for repression. The subsequent impossibility of using the language in public social spaces imposed a withdrawal of Euskara into the more personal confines of private life and the family. And this intimate environment thus became the privileged space of its basic use (See Section 2, Chapter 5).

ADDED TO this repression of the language in official spheres and public spaces, a demographically important immigration process took place in the 1950s and 1960s (see Section 1, Chapter 3) and the result of all this was a decline in Basque-language use, both in terms of geographical space and social environment.

AT THE SAME time as the repression was taking place, and as a response to it, during the initial years of the post–Spanish Civil War era, in seminaries and other religious institutions, the task of recovering Basque and Basque literature took place silently (see Section 2, Chapter 9). Years later, this would encourage a socially significant cultural recovery, a cultural renaissance evident in five different fields.[38] It laid the foundations for Euskara's unification, modernization, and normalization. It promoted, above all from about 1960 onward, the project of Basque schools, with the creation of *ikastolas* using the Basque language as a vehicle of communication and thus breaking the secular isolation between Euskara and the school, (see Section 2, Chapter 7). In 1966, a Basque-language adult literacy movement emerged (see Section 3, Chapter 14) with a twofold objective: to teach Basque speakers to read and to write in Euskara and to promote the language among sectors of the public who did not speak it. The linguistic recovery process would take most recognizable shape through the important development and renovation of several literary fields in Basque. Finally, the attempt to transform Euskara in order to adapt it to the needs of modern industrial urban society would lead it to addressing entirely new fields, fields such as scientific knowledge that had, until that time, remained almost completely out of its realm.

EUSKARA AS A POLITICAL SYMBOL

In time, this process of linguistic and cultural recovery coincided with a redefinition of the Basque national consciousness. This idea—that language might constitute the foundation of the Basque nation—ultimately led to a discarding of other elements on which identifying

Guardians of the language
The head office of Euskaltzaindia (the Academy of the Basque Language), Bilbao, Bizkaia. Created in 1919, the academy was established to aid the development and promotion of Euskara.
Photo: Iñaki Martínez de Albeniz.

Basque difference had rested. And gradually it came to be seen that nationality, or the differential nature of the Basque people, could not fall back on biological arguments (race). Consequently, Basque nationalism redefined itself in the 1960s on this ideological reformulation, and as a result, the language acquired a preeminent position as *the* basic component, above all others, of Basque collective identity.

The language was thus transformed into the empirical equivalent of the Basque people's differential identity. However, what was most telling was the fact that, as knowledge of the language grew, so did a collective sense of Basque national identity. And the more the language was encouraged and promoted, this identity acquired greater influence. As such, there was a growing connection between the Basque language and Basque nationalism. And in every (more or less successful) attempt to redefine Basque nationalism to this day, a special place has always been reserved for the language, to the extent that there is a noticeably strong link between the discourse of Basque nationalist demands and those of recovering the language.

When a community defines itself in terms of being a national political community, language can acquire a political value. This has certainly been the case where a language has been presented, before members of the social group, as the national language. Guy Rocher argues that symbols occupy, evoke, or even take the place of other words or concepts. [39] It is, surely, no coincidence then that social groups identify themselves as speakers of a certain language. Indeed, in Euskara, the same word expresses being Basque and speaking the language: *euskaldun*.

LANGUAGE might thus acquire symbolic value for a group of individuals. Because it is of such symbolic value, it is not necessary to know it, but only to accept that value in a sort of affective relationship with the symbol, since such support symbolizes before other actors a degree of participation in the collectivity. In this way, one can begin to understand how an element that is not shared—or rather, a communicative code that is not possessed—by all the members of a given society can still become a defining element for that whole community. Affective support for the symbol is a form of possessing it. In the collective representation that Basque nationalists maintained through their community, language became an "objective" feature as an element that permitted the identification of the differential nature of the Basque collective. This in turn led to a separation between symbolic dimensions of language—identification with it—and the communicative use of it. In other words, in the former case, it is a question of using the language as a symbol of belonging to a linguistic, social, or national community through support for the language symbolizing support for the community, while in the latter case, language is a means of communicative interaction.

THERE IS, however, a big difference between the level of symbolic acceptance for the language as the symbol of the Basque community and the level of comprehension and/or use of Euskara on the other. The symbolic value of the language, through numerous examples, was prior to that of its Basque nationalist interpretation. Yet through Basque nationalism, the language embraced, beyond just its social value as a symbol of belonging to a community of individuals, a political dimension. From then on, the Basque nationalist and pro-Basque language movements were inextricably linked, to the point of almost creating a total identification between the symbolic dimension and political consciousness.

However, just as symbolic appreciation had previously significantly influenced language use, political consciousness also became an important factor in encouraging the learning and use of the language. For those social actors who had developed such political consciousness, this became a motivation with major consequences. Thus, in the late 1970s, there was a significant growth in the number of people wanting to learn Euskara, leading many of them to attend night schools and *euskaltegis* (special centers dedicated to adult learning of Basque) (see Section 3, Chapter 14). At that time, demand outweighed the material and human possibilities of supply. Through a great deal of volunteerism, an attempt was made to respond to the avalanche of interest that, in the language world, came to be regarded as Euskara's "boom" moment. The causes of this were many and varied, but, without a doubt, political motivation was a powerfully strong influence. Its role, though, was reinforced by several other very relevant and no less socially significant factors.

Lesson ten

LEARNING OBJECTIVES

1. To understand the main figures involved in promoting the growing link between Euskara and Basque identity.
2. To understand the key historical, sociostructural, and political reasons for the decline of Euskara.
3. To differentiate between the communicative and participative function of a language, or its symbolic and functional components.
4. To examine the relationship between the Basque language and Basque nationalism.

REQUIRED READING

Joshua A. Fishman, *Language and Ethnicity in Minority Sociolinguistic Perspective* (Clevedon, England: Multilingual Matters, 1989).

Benjamín Tejerina, "Language and Basque Nationalism: Collective Identity, Social Conflict and Institutionalization," in *Nationalism and the Nation in the Iberian Peninsula: Competing and Conflicting Identities*, ed. Clare Mar-Molinero and Angel Smith (Oxford: Berg, 1996), 221–36.

SUGGESTED READING

Gobierno Vasco, *II Encuesta sociolingüística de Euskal Herria 1996: La continuidad del Euskara II* (Vitoria-Gasteiz: Servicio Central de Publicaciones del Gobierno Vasco, 1999).

Benjamín Tejerina, *Nacionalismo y lengua: Los procesos de cambio lingüístico en el País Vasco* (Madrid: CIS-Siglo XXI, 1992).

WRITTEN LESSON FOR SUBMISSION

1. How did language and identity come to be identified with one another in the Basque Country?
2. What values do social actors attribute to language? Do you know of any other cases where language has become an identity symbol for a whole society?

Igor Ahedo

11 · Political parties
in the Basque autonomous community

SUMMARY
Using categories borrowed from political science, the present chapter analyzes the political party system in the Basque Autonomous Community. Reproducing the social plurality typical of a modern society, the Basque political system does not just display class differences, but also displays an identity-based dimension that divides Basque nationalist from non-Basque nationalist parties. Taking account of the typical indicators that mark political rhythms, what follows also offers a descriptive overview of the main political formations and the system of alliances that shaped institutional politics from 1980 to 2001.

AMONG THE various typologies of party systems that allow one to categorize political units, one of the most frequently used was devised by Giovanni Sartori.[40] Taking note of electoral power and the existing level of polarization—or the ideological distance separating formations—he establishes a theory that differentiates between single-party, hegemonic-party, predominant-party, two-party, limited moderate multiparty, and extreme polarized multiparty systems. Thus, for example, American model is characterized by a clear two-party tendency between Republicans and Democrats, but the political system of the Basque Autonomous Community (BAC) displays all the features of an extreme polarized multiparty system. This is due to the fact that there are six relevant parties marked by considerable ideological distances between one another, and that gives rise to bilateral oppositions and a centripetal multipolar competition.

Traditionally, the bipolar party system has been marked by a concentration of different formations based on class cleavages. However, beyond mere ideology, in the Basque Country, there are also other lines of cleavage, among which one might highlight that shaped by the different identities that these different formations assume.[41] The intersection of these two dimensions—ideological and identity-based—has produced the current extreme polarized multiparty system in the BAC. However, the importance of this conflict over identity has also strengthened centripetal trends that draw together different formations into two unmistakable sectors: Basque and non-Basque nationalists.

The center-right Partido Nacionalista Vasco (PNV, Basque Nationalist Party), the social-democratic Eusko Alkartasuna (EA, Basque Solidarity), and the radical nationalist Herri Batasuna (HB, Popular Unity) compete within the Basque nationalist sphere. The social-democratic Partido Socialista de Euskadi (PSE, Basque Socialist Party), a branch of the Partido Socialista Obrero Español (PSOE, Spanish Socialist Workers Party), and the center-right Partido Popular (PP, Popular Party) classify themselves within the non-Basque nationalist sphere.

THE PNV WAS formed in 1898 by Sabino Arana. After an initial pro-independence phase (1898–1914) the party toned down its discourse, accepting a statute of autonomy during the Spanish Civil War in 1937. On the losing side at the close of the war in 1939, the now-exiled PNV concentrated on diplomatic lobbying to secure the downfall of the Franco dictatorship, abandoning open political activity within the Basque Country itself as a result of the repressive nature of the regime.

After the death of Franco in 1975, the PNV kept its distance from the process associated with the reform of the Spanish state, encouraging a vote of abstention in the

Corridors of power
Sabin Etxea, the head office of the PNV (Partido Nacionalista Vasco, Basque Nationalist Party), Bilbao, Bizkaia. Despite its modern façade, one can still observe remnants of the building's origins, built in the traditional style of a Basque farmstead.
Photo: Iñaki Martínez de Albeniz.

1978 referendum on the new Spanish Constitution. However, it did fully support the Statute of Autonomy (the Statute of Gernika) for the Basque Autonomous Community in 1979. Thus, the PNV has participated from 1980 to this day in controlling the Basque Autonomous Government, at first alone and, since the mid-1980s, in various coalitions.

A sector within the PNV split away from the party in 1986 to form EA. This was the result of a series of internal disputes, together with this sector's more social-democratic leanings and clear support for self-determination. After overcoming their original differences, and in part as a consequence of waning support for EA and the gradual recovery of the PNV (see Table 26), the two parties subsequently formed an alliance to guarantee Basque nationalist hegemony in the Basque institutions.

THE FAILURE of traditional Basque nationalism to respond adequately to Franco's repression of the Basque language, culture, and history led to the creation of ETA (Euskadi 'ta Askatasuna, Basque Homeland and Freedom) in 1959, a group that began to use political violence in 1968. It adopted a Marxist ideological stance, calling for outright independence and the reunification of all Basque provinces on both sides of the French-Spanish border. However, because the clandestine nature of ETA prevented it from taking direct part in politics, HB was formed in 1978. This party was joined by other social movements—in defense of the language, for example, or antirepression collectives—in developing both an electoral and an institutional strategy. Together, these collectives formed the self-styled Movimiento de Liberación Nacional Vasco (MLNV, the Movement for Basque National Liberation) and soon created a pyramidal organizational model. At the top of this pyramid was a nucleus formed by a small group of activists making up the coordinating group, Koordinadora Abertzale Sozialista (KAS, the Socialist Nationalist Coordinating Council), underneath which were various sectors and groups, and at the base, HB. Despite this, ETA had set itself up as intrinsically against the Spanish state, to which the legitimizing community of this antisystem Basque nationalism was forced to conform. It therefore implied a symbolic hierarchy that has explained the incapacity of HB to distance itself from ETA.[42]

The PSOE has sustained its historical strength in the BAC through the support of certain geographical enclaves that experienced major industrialization and high immigration rates during the second half of the last century. Originally it maintained a discourse that allowed it to approach the position of moderate Basque nationalism (formerly supporting, for example, the right of self-determination for the Basque Country), but from the mid 1970s onward, it began to advocate a more pro-autonomy line. Indeed, after its rise to power at the Spanish state level in 1982, it was charged with overseeing this autonomy process throughout the state. In the Basque Country, the incorporation of Euskadiko Ezkerra (EE, the Basque Left)—originally a breakaway faction from ETA and specifically its politico-military wing, known as ETA (pm)—into the PSE in 1990 resulted in a pro-Basque shift within the party. This in turn led to its participation in the Basque government alongside Basque nationalists and also accounted for a significant increase in electoral support.

THE PP STARTED out in the BAC in 1990 under the leadership of Jaime Mayor Oreja, the later minister of the interior in the central Spanish government. Until that time the traditionalist right-wing, inheritor of the Franco regime's political debts, had been organized around the electorally weak Alianza Popular (AP, the Popular Alliance). However, a crisis in the centrist Unión de Centro Democrático (UCD, Union of the Democratic Center), a party that enjoyed significant support in the Basque Country, served as a springboard for the right wing to reform in the mid-1990s around the PP with the ultimate goal of ending Basque nationalist hegemony in the BAC. At the same time, this new political landscape was also marked by a high degree of tension provoked

Table 25

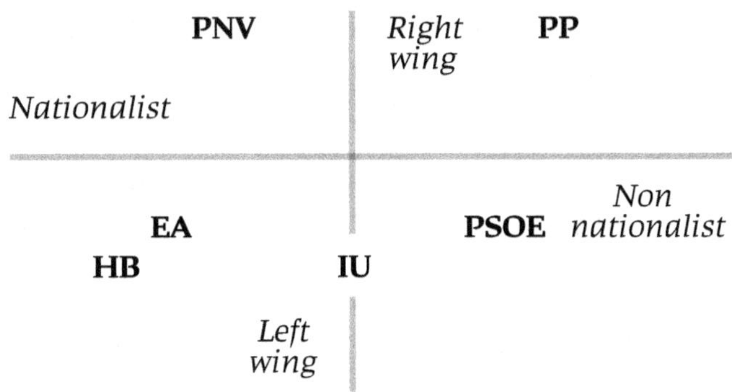

The ideological and identity-based spectrum of Basque political parties

There are two clear dimensions to Basque political parties: ideology, with parties embracing right-wing, left-wing, and centrist positions, and identity, with parties emphasizing their Basque or Spanish nature.

Parallel to these two clearly defined poles, which are evident in a series of institutional coalitions (at the Basque, provincial, and municipal government levels), there are two left-wing formations: the previously mentioned HB, an antisystem Basque nationalist group, and Izquierda Unida (IU, United Left), a communist party that argues for a federal Spanish state model. This table approximates the position of all the groups within the matrix of these ideological and identity-based poles.

by the brutality of ETA assassinations and, at the state level, a serious crisis within the PSOE.[43]

THE DEVELOPMENT OF POLITICAL PARTIES

From the mid-1980s through to the mid-1990s, there was broad consensus among all Basque political parties, with the exception of the radical Basque nationalists (HB), based on two main principles. First, he PSOE promised to renew the process of transferring powers to the BAC, which had been suspended since 1981. The second was a pacification policy that hinged on the so-called Ajuria-Enea Pact of 1988. Among its ten points, sponsored by the Basque nationalist *lehendakari*, José Antonio Ardanza, and supported by all parties except HB, it emphasized that political issues should be dealt with only by political parties and that the problem of violence should be addressed by standard policing methods, combined with a policy of social reinsertion for ETA members who gave up the armed struggle.

THIS TWOFOLD compromise implied the full participation of the PSE-PSOE in the Basque government alongside Basque nationalists. However, in the mid-1990s, agreement on both principles collapsed due to the continued suspension of the process of transferring powers, and a U-turn on the part of the Spanish government as regards Basque fiscal autonomy (and in particular the Fiscal Pact) was evident. The PNV then began to look for a new pacification policy, resulting in it adopting a strategy that would ultimately define the conflict in purely political—and therefore not just police—terms.

In sum, through to the late 1990s and originating in the Ajuria-Enea Pact, there appeared to be majority consensus among all Basque parties in drawing a line between so-called "democratic" and "violent" political

The public face of politics
A scene depicting the space between the institutional and the quotidian in the political life of the Basque Autonomous Community. The banner urges people to "make independence and socialism," a typical slogan of radical Basque nationalism.
Photo: Iñaki Martínez de Albeniz.

---

actors, evinced by the marginalization of HB from Basque political life.

HOWEVER, developments since 1998 have resulted in a fault line that, although always present, has led to the polarization of the Basque political system into two new centripetal vectors: Basque nationalist and constitutionalist parties, with the latter regarding the Spanish Constitution, and the Statute of Gernika that came out of it, as the fundamental benchmark from which Basque political autonomy should be guided.

Table 26

	1980	1984	1986
PNV	349,102	451,178	271,701
EA	0	0	181,175
PNV-EA	0	0	0
HB	151,636	157,389	199,900
Basque Nationalists	595,971	704,952	776,706
PSOE-PSE	130,221	247,786	252,233
PP	43,751	100,581	55,606
Consti-tutionalists	319,304	368,626	367,326
IU	0	0	0

	1990	1994	1998	2001
PNV	289,701	304,346	347,968	0
EA	115,703	105,135	108,607	0
PNV-EA	0	0	0	604,222
HB	186,147	166,147	223,264	143,139
Basque Nationalists	670,919	575,629	679,829	747,361
PSOE-PSE	202,736	174,682	218,607	253,195
PP	83,719	146,960	250,580	326,933
Consti-tutionalists	331,549	416,395	548,929	588,046
IU	14,351	27,797	15,782	78,862

Votes cast for the main political parties in the Basque Autonomous Community, 1980–2001
A summary of the votes obtained by the main Basque political parties in different elections between 1980 and 2001.
Source: Author's calculation.

THE ELECTORAL DEVELOPMENT OF BASQUE PARTIES

Table 26 shows the electoral results, in terms of total votes gained, of the most important parties in the BAC. Using this information, one might summarize the key landmarks in the development of the Basque political system.

The PNV has been the hegemonic party in the BAC throughout this period, receiving its greatest number of votes just prior to the split with EA, after which it initially lost support, only to recover it later. This was the opposite of the EA trend, which, coupled with the rise in support for constitutionalist parties, resulted in it entering into a coalition with the PNV in 2001.

That same year marked the lowest level of electoral support for HB. In 1986, it attained nearly two hundred thousand votes, a figure it bettered only during the ETA ceasefire of 1998. However, ETA's return to arms resulted in a loss of 40 percent of support for HB, a decline that helped the Spanish government (led by the PP) to outlaw this party in 2002.

The PSOE was the hegemonic non-Basque nationalist force between 1980 and 1998, but gradually lost ground from 1990 onward, the year in which the PP was created.

A NEW POLITICAL scenario emerged in 1998, involving breaking the former consensus of a commonly agreed pacification policy and the development of the autonomy statute. As can be seen, there was a massive turnout: Basque nationalist parties gained more than one hundred thousand more votes than in previous elections, and the constitutionalists gained one hundred and fifty thousand.

However, the PP and PSOE strategy also served as an incentive to mobilize sectors that previously had abstained from voting. And although sociological studies predicted that these people would lend their support to the PP or the PSOE in 2001, the results demonstrated that the constitutionalist faction seemed to have reached its electoral limit (gaining only forty thousand votes), while Basque nationalism in general grew despite the spectacular fall of HB (which lost seventy thousand). One should also take note of the spectacular rise of IU which not only distanced itself from the constitutionalist sector, but actually joined the Basque government coalition after the elections.

IN SUM, the Basque political system demonstrates a clear multiparty structure deriving from the intersection of ideological and identity-based dimensions. It seems to have reshaped itself gradually around two centripetal coalitions defined by the relationship they envisage between the Basque Country and the Spanish state.

Lesson eleven

LEARNING OBJECTIVES

1. To understand the main characteristics of the party system in the Basque Autonomous Community.
2. To understand the nationalist issue and its expression through political parties as another component of classifying party systems.
3. To develop a basic understanding of each of the principal political parties in the Basque Autonomous Community.
4. To develop an overview of Basque political parties in terms of their respective electoral fortunes.

REQUIRED READING

Francisco Letamendia, *Game of Mirrors: Centre-Periphery National Conflicts* (London: Ashgate, 2000).

Francisco Llera, "Basque Polarization: Between Autonomy and Independence," in *Identity and Territorial Autonomy in Plural Societies*, ed. William Safran and Ramón Máiz (Boulder, Colo.: Frank Cass Publishers, 2000), 101–20.

SUGGESTED READING

William A. Douglass, Carmelo Urza, Linda White, and Joseba Zulaika, eds., *Basque Politics and Nationalism on the Eve of the Millennium* (Reno: Basque Studies Program, 1999).

Stein Rokkan, *Citizens, Elections, Parties* (Oslo: Universitetsforlaget, 1970).

WRITTEN LESSON FOR SUBMISSION

1. Choose any Basque political party, examine its origins, and analyze its current characteristics.
2. Critically assess the relationship between ethnic or peripheral nationalism and party systems. Illustrate your answer with examples from the Basque case.

Benjamín Tejerina

12 · Civil society and social movements

SUMMARY

Located somewhere between the social and the political, the cultural and the institutional, social movements are truly innovative centers in society and politics. In this exploration of social movements in the Basque Country, in addition to examining the issue theoretically, we will also briefly look at the nature of the activists themselves, as well as these groups' organizational structure and operation and their strategies of alliance and opposition.

STUDIES of the new social movements have emphasized two aspects that are not always clearly differentiated: their political and sociocultural dimensions. Every social movement tries to maintain a balance between its ethical conviction (at a sociocultural level) and its logic of efficiency (its political activity). According to Claus Offe, "the new social movements try to politicize the institutions of civil society in such a way as to not be constrained by the channels of political institutions. In order to free themselves from the state, they have to politicize civil society itself ... through strategies which are located somewhere between, on the one hand, 'private' concerns and issues and, on the other, institutional political activity sanctioned by the state."[44]

Faced with this perspective accentuating the more political dimension of social movements, other observers prefer to focus on their social or cultural aspects. Alberto Melucci clearly represents this position in criticizing those who, as he sees it, fall into political reductionism by considering both old and new social movements as solely political: "this reductionism leaves out the issue of structural change in complex societies and underestimates the great importance of social and cultural dimensions in contemporary collective activity." According to Melucci, one should also look for the social roots of political activity: "if the foundation of contemporary conflicts has shifted towards the production of meaning, then apparently they have little to do with politics. These movements' activity is pre-political because it is rooted in the experiences of everyday life; and meta-political because political factions can never completely represent them."[45]

Where there does appear to be a certain concurrence among these different perspectives, however, is in their agreement that social movements imply a strengthening of the public space and a revitalizing of civil society.[46] According to Offe, "the new paradigm [in which new social movements are located] divides the universe of action into three spheres (private / against noninstitutional politics / against institutional politics) and claims a sphere of 'political activity inside civil society' as its own space from which to question both private and politico-institutional practices and institutions."[47]

SOCIAL movements and their consequences are located at the point between the sphere of institutional reality and that of society, with its multiple social actors and varied organizations. With their complex and at times contradictory internal factions, social movements are privileged agents of social and (especially) of institutional change. Within the institutional sphere, one should differentiate between basic political agents (the public administrations of state and political parties) and institutions that do not have political goals. It is toward the first of these that most social move-ments direct or focus their activity. It is sometimes more difficult to establish a clear differentiation between political parties and social movements. This is

Politics and society
The Artekale Batzoki, Bilbao. Batzokis, bar-restaurants affiliated to the PNV (Partido Nacionalista Vasco, Basque Nationalist Party), serve as social meeting spaces for sympathizers of this party.
Photo: Iñaki Martínez de Albeniz.

---

because, on the one hand, there are political parties whose organizational one hand, there are political parties whose organizational characteristics and functioning (such is the case with some nationalist parties and organizations, and certain minority or extraparliamentary parties) resemble traditional forms of social movements, and on the other, because, on reaching a certain organizational threshold and taking definitive shape, some social movements turn into political parties (green parties, religious parties, and so on).

A social movement is not one specific thing in social reality. Nor does it behave, except occasionally, as an actor or collective subject. In the same way as an institution, organization, or society, it is the result of a multiplicity of interactions. One might therefore define a social movement as the result of collective activity (or a collective challenge) made up of the combined set of formal and informal interactions. A social movement is maintained by a plurality of organized individuals, collectives, and groups who share, to a greater or lesser extent, the feeling of collective belonging or identity, and further by the interactive structures that are established with other social or political agents with whom they compete for the appropriation of, participation in, or transformation of power relations or social objectives to be attained through the mobilization of certain sectors of society.

SOCIAL ACTIVISTS IN THE BASQUE COUNTRY

THE ACTIVISTS in Basque social movements belong to two generations: those aged over forty who have been active for many years and recent arrivals who are mostly under thirty-five years of age. The youngest activists largely come from sectors close to the Catholic Church, from the world of pressure groups and associations, and, in some cases, from left-wing Basque nationalist sectors. Most of the older activists previously took part in organizations associated with other movements and include those whose participation began during the transition to democracy (1975–80). The activists who have remained the longest in social movements are those who experienced their political socialization toward the end of the Franco regime or in the immediate aftermath of his death (see Section 3, Chapter 15).

Previous political activity by activists helps their integration into an organization, since it makes the socialization process less complex. The integration process of activists who come from the political world is easier than for those who do not have any previous political experience. The most typical recruitment mechanisms are those of personal-relationship networks, related political organizations, and the personal experience of discrimination or injustice. The existence of personal-relationship networks makes integration into the group less protracted. Similarly, the fact of having belonged to more or less similar political organizations from an ideological perspective provides "cultural baselines" that allow activists to interpret reality in a certain shared way. And needless to say, the experience of discrimination or injustice can be a significant motivator to political activity. In particular, certain moments of exceptional political mobilization, such as the sociopolitical context experienced during the transition, stimulated the activism of many people. However, what has come to be known as the privatization of life has limited the potential mobilization of social movements, because it reduces one's personal commitment to the causes defended by social movements and to political participation in general.

THE MOST committed activists within their organizations (the leaders) belong to the new middle classes and are especially linked to universities, being professionals in the social and cultural services sector. There is no significant blue-collar presence, while there is a strong incidence of university students and unemployed youth.

ORGANIZATIONAL STRUCTURE AND FUNCTIONING

Taking into consideration the territorial location and distribution of these different organizations, one might categorize three types of groups: those with a national projection, those that operate in autonomous fashion or in a markedly local way, and coordinating organizations.

Organizations with a national projection tend to be represented throughout the Basque Autonomous Community, displaying a markedly ideological nature or expecting to monopolize the movement. The second organizational type is formed by those groups that lack any clear ideological bond with political organizations and that have little power within the corresponding movement. However, they have understood how to strengthen themselves by virtue of specializing in one specific dimension of an issue. Finally, there are those organizations that constitute a conglomeration of groups, coordinating organizations that take on board multiple organizations and try to bring together the whole social movement.

FROM AN organizational perspective, all such social movements are characterized by a high degree of fragmentation and also by the proliferation of groups that respond, in some cases, to a process of ideologically based internal division, and in others, to a process of strategic diversification or growing specialization. Although coordination attempts between organizations encounter serious difficulties, they are still interesting processes for the movement itself, for civil society, and for the public administration. The coordinators of groups and collectives allow an organizational and ideological pluralism while at the same time facilitating a unity of permanent or specific activity through a major economy of material, human, and organizational resources. This coordination allows the movement to express itself with a single voice and to be perceived as such by civil society, making collaboration and negotiation with the public administration less costly. Judged either way, the existence of coordinating organizations reinforces the negotiating role of social movements in their sphere of activity, thus facilitating negotiation and conflict resolution.

The internal structure of social movements also displays significant differences. There are organizations that have adopted more formal models, with an elaborate and clearly stated structure and of a generally hierarchical nature that in turn allows a certain swiftness in decision making or in fulfilling instructions. Most of these organizations have an administrative infrastructure formed by full-time activists. At the other extreme there are those organizations whose internal infrastructure is less formal, without a structure that is reflected in the everyday dynamic of the collective. Instead, members tend to create informal groups based on personal and friendship ties, and the organization receives its shape from the type of activists it has.

HETEROGENEITY between the organizations also influences their decision making and internal working. As a general rule, there exist two operational models that, although different, appear related in several ways within some organizations. The assembly model is characterized by the search for unanimity and consensus in decision making. This search for consensus often leads to a progressive sidelining of more conflictive issues for fear of provoking internal division. This decision-making process implies rejecting permanent forms of representation or delegation and frequently becomes an ideological feature of the organization. Such a structure allows for the appearance of informal leaderships that operate in more or less explicit form. The organizations that adopt delegated forms of representation are a response to the other model, which seeks a more efficient means of mobilization.

Almost every group has a similar decision-making process: a commission-based operation regarding the specialization of debate in different spheres of activity, a general assembly that follows a voting system, and a

Social activism
An image of institutionalized environmentalism. A bookstore and meeting point of the environmental action group Ekologistak Martxan (Ecologists in Action) in Bilbao's old quarter. Nongovernmental organizations and social movements occupy an important place in Basque society.
Photo: Iñaki Martínez de Albeniz.

---

smaller permanent commission that is the representative and decision-making organ between the different assemblies. The greater presence throughout the geographical area of the Basque Country an organization has, this basic outline becomes more complex, with the addition of area or regional coordinating organisms. This model is based on the explicit acceptance and recognition of internal and leadership plurality in the organization, although this doesn't mean that it is always respected. In general terms, one might argue that within more formal structures, the permanent commission is an organ within which an important amount of power is concentrated, resulting in a high degree of control.

THE MOST typical sources of finance are activists' and participants' dues, together with the sale of diverse material: informative journals, calendars, T-shirts, and so on. Most organizations accept official subsidies, although some refuse this type of aid because they consider it negative, believing that economic dependence may introduce a distorting element into their autonomous organizational functioning. The lack of sufficiently consistent financing channels is a serious impediment to both activity and potential activity and affects the organizations of all social movements.

ORGANIZATIONAL STRATEGIES

The classic distinctions between potential strategies to be adopted by organizations in social movements suggests that some gravitate toward power, focusing on the results of political decision making and the distribution of power and following a logic of instrumental action. Other organizations, however, follow an expressive logic of action that fits a strategy oriented toward identity, "which points to cultural codes, behavior consistent with roles, self-fulfillment, personal identity, authenticity."[48] Although one kind of strategy almost always tends to predominate over another, in almost every organization there is a combination of both logics, both in specific groups of activists and in the types of activities they develop. This boundary between instrumental and expressive logic has become more and more blurred in contemporary social movements. As Melucci points out,

> movements function before the rest of society like a separate medium class whose principal purpose is to

> bring to light what the system itself doesn't say; the share of silence, violence or chance that always underscores dominant codes. These movements are means which speak to us through action. ... Therefore, their activity takes place in the sphere of symbols and communication. All this cancels out the old distinction between the instrumental and expressive meaning of action, because in the experience of contemporary movements, the results of their activity and the individual experience of new codes tend to coincide.[49]

THE IMPORTANT thing is not so much whether or not differences exist between groups as regards the strategy shaping their activity, but rather the way that social factors promote the predominance of one or the other logic. One of the first variable factors is found in the objectives pursued that shape instrumental activity toward either negotiation with the institutions or toward confrontation with the system. The degree of radicalism in groups' political and ideological arguments is a second factor influencing the strategy adopted: moderation in the transformation mechanisms through participation or the radical search for contradictions through a strategy of civil disobedience, using official repression as a delegitimizing element of power and a legitimizing one for the movement before society as a whole. A third factor leading to significant differences concerns the movement's organizational structure, facilitating conflict or cooperation in different degrees. Faced with internal and external conflict, an inflexible organizational structure frequently will lead to organizational fragmentation (environmental and ethnolinguistic movements, for example), while flexible structures facilitate group specialization (feminist movements). A fourth factor is the level of adaptation between organizational structure and

Environmentalism in action

A poster announcing a demonstration against proposals for a new high-speed railroad system in the Basque Country.

Image by courtesy of AHT Gelditu! Elkarlana.

types of activist. In a situation of organizational pluralism, there is a close relationship between certain characteristics of the activists and certain organizational forms, which in turn allows for a growing specialization and professionalization, as in the cases of the ethnolinguistic movement or feminist activity. Changes in the political realm usually also lead to important consequences for the strategy chosen by an organization or movement. The feminist, environmentalist, and ethnolinguistic movements demonstrate how, as some of their goals or demands are institutionalized, a reflection takes place that leads ultimately to a strategic change. The structure of political opportunity has an important influence on the strategy and results of the collective activity undertaken by these social movements.

SOCIAL MOVEMENTS, POLITICS, AND THE STATE

An important aspect for the success of these movements is accessibility to the political decision-making sphere. A decentralized state offers more opportunities for such access than a strongly centralized one. This element was especially important in the strategy pursued by the antimilitarist movement, which involved local bodies in its refusal to do obligatory military service or conscription. Many groups' geographical organization and activity in markedly local environments also facilitates and stimulates this dynamic, putting pressure on local administrations closer to the average citizen. The same might also be said for provincial and autonomous institutions that are more accessible to the strategy of social movements.

ACCESSIBILITY must be combined, however, with a predisposition to allow the expression of social conflicts. The demands of social movements indicate the existence of real conflicts, but the groups that control political power have a series of potential responses at their disposal. Attempts to solve conflicts at root level usually receive coercive responses, while gaining recognition of the legitimacy of collective action involves using controlling measures and a degree of institutionalization. This latter approach seems more effective from the perspective of those in power and is more difficult to counteract on the part of social movements, as the feminist and environmental cases demonstrate. On the other hand, the use of repressive measures, whether indiscriminately or selectively, can actually increase the legitimacy of movements' demands and contribute to the delegitimizing of their adversaries, as was the case with the ethnolinguistic and antimilitarist movements.

GIVEN THE organizational fragmentation of social movements and the difficulty of evaluating the multiple relations between each organization and the public administrations, it would be interesting to explore the dynamic relationship between a social movement and a more stable political structure: the multi-organizational terrain of the movement. Because general practice suggests that the state feels tempted to use more repressive methods against weaker contenders, it would seem logical that social movements can act in a reverse way: To the extent that members can be protected by a relationship network with other groups and collectives that will help them in times of crisis, it is possible to envisage more radical strategies accentuating the contradictions within the coalition in power, as has been the case with the civil disobedience employed by the antimilitarist movement.

Attempting to expand the number of one's allies and to reduce the number of one's opponents are the goals of any organization. The alliance system that every group tries to secure implicates other groups from the same or different movements, together with ideologically varied political organizations. In certain cases, groups seek help in extraparliamentary left-wing organizations or from the radical Basque nationalist world. The interactive structure between these groups is based on ideological interpersonal relations, out of which a not always stable alliance emerges. These alliance systems establish interactive relationships between organizations in the same movement, with basic agents in the political sphere, political parties, and institutions, yet also with a multiplicity of groups and collectives in civil society.

AT THE SAME time that an organization establishes an alliance system, it also shapes a conflict system with the collectives that compete for the same objective and disposable resources or that even act against the organization itself. These conflictive relations can affect organizations in the same movement or opposing sectors in a specific group, such as conflicts within the pacifist, environmental, feminist and ethnolinguistic movements that have ended in organizational fragmentation or even in the abandonment of activism. Yet they can also implicate political parties (environmentalists against Euskalerriko Berdeak, Basque Green Party, and pacifists against the radical nationalist party HB, for example) and public administrations (antisystem groups). It is almost unavoidable for an alliance system to take shape without also shaping a conflictive system with collectives at a significant ideological distance.

Lesson twelve

LEARNING OBJECTIVES

1. To understand the plural nature of social movements.
2. To analyze why social movements pursue certain strategies.

---

3. To understand the influence of the historical context on the existence of different generations of activists.
4. To contextualize the preceding objectives within the framework of the contemporary Basque Country.

REQUIRED READING

Benjamín Tejerina, "Cycles of Protest, Social Movements and Political Violence in the Basque Country," *Nations and Nationalism* 7, no. 1 (2001): 39–57.

Cyrus Ernesto Zirakzadeh, *A Rebellious People: Basques, Protests, and Politics* (Reno: University of Nevada Press, 1991), 53–79.

SUGGESTED READING

Alberto Melucci, *Challenging Codes: Collective Action in the Information Age* (Cambridge: Cambridge University Press, 1996).

Claus Offe, "Challenging the Boundaries of Institutional Politics: Social Movements Since the 1960s," in *Changing Boundaries of the Political: Essays on the Evolving Balance between the State and Society, Public and Private in Europe*, ed. Charles Maier (Cambridge, Cambridge University Press, 1987), 63–107.

WRITTEN LESSON FOR SUBMISSION

1. Choose one Basque social movement, examine its origin, and analyze this in terms of the theoretical elements described above.
2. What specific changes in the relationship between politics and society have led to the proliferation of social movements?

Section 3: Identity, culture, and everyday life

Iñaki Martínez de Albeniz

13 · Nationalism in the Basque Country

Transformation and political crisis

SUMMARY

The era of political institutionalization beginning with the Statute of Gernika in 1979 was a decisive moment for the Basque Country. The goals of this chapter are to describe the historical development of Basque nationalism and to evaluate the changes that the passing of the statute implied for Basque politics. These changes are debated within the framework of two opposing sociological arguments: one that contends political institutionalization led to a depoliticizing of society and another asserting, on the contrary, that it resulted in the politicization of certain sectors of society (the private, work, and cultural spheres for example) and features of identity (age, gender, and so on) that were previously not considered political or even susceptible to politicization. The latter argument rests on a postmodern perspective that calls for the extension, or at least reconstruction, of political confines, thereby leading to a new kind of political identity and opening up to analysis identification processes that go beyond conventional political identities.

AT ROOT, the process of political institutionalization that began after the passing of the Statute of Gernika in 1979 shaped the transformation of the earlier forms of sociopolitical reproduction and integration associated with the authoritarian regime (political control of the whole social sphere) into an autonomous, democratic society (see Section 1, Chapter 2). This meant overcoming a model of political articulation—dominant during the Franco era—that, as has been seen in previous chapters (see Section 2), was defined by the several related features. These included political control of the public sphere and the reduction of the processes of political reproduction and socialization to the private sphere. The streets thus became a privileged political space in which to answer the regime (above all during Franco's later years), while at the same time, politics became central to people's lifeworlds. In other words, people became dedicated to politics. This included a unanimously political evaluation of the Basque language. Violence also became a central reference point of politics.

BY CONTRAST, the predominant model that prevailed after the institutionalization process was defined by the emergence of a public sphere of legitimation and democratic expression that featured the reproduction and socialization of consciousness in both public and private spheres. Democratic political institutions suddenly appeared as the privileged site of politics, while cultural and linguistic development became topics of public debate. At the same time, politics itself became less central, and a variety of ways to evaluate the Basque language—political, cultural, pragmatic—came into play. There was a rational rejection of violence.

Each of these two models implies a different logic and dynamic, but the term "political institutionalization" should not be understood merely as the transformation process by which the second model fully replaced the first. What has made the Basque political situation complex during the last three decades is that the logics of both models have, in fact, coexisted, even though it is true that the relative strength and legitimacy of each is not the same (see Section 1, Chapter 2). The basic difference between the two models is that the second (termed "political institutionalization") has imposed greater privatism, plurality, and tolerance in public-political life, to the point of implying the full incorporation of the Basque Country in modernity's rationalization process.

And one elemental feature of this process is that politics has become a specialized and increasingly professional activity. However, the first model survives in some concentrated areas of Basque society, implying that the political opinion previously dominant during the Franco regime, which considered political transformations associated with the political institutionalization process irrelevant, still exists for a significant part of the Basque population.

To this dual dynamic one should add, moreover, a third vector of change, "the crisis of conventional politics and advent of new politicizations." This complicates the situation even further if applied to the contemporary political map of the Basque Country.

I WILL SYNTHESIZE these three forms of experiencing and thinking about politics in the Basque Country through what I believe to be an illustrative play on words. For those who, despite the coming of a democratic political regime, remain attached to a political opinion shaped during the Franco system, *politics is everything.* That is, politics continues, as was previously the case, to shelter their entire day-to-day existence and give it meaning (or meaninglessness, depending on how one views it). For their part, however, for those who participated in the process of political institutionalization process, now *politics isn't everything:* Having become a professional career, politics has become one more reality within an everyday spectrum that includes other dimensions of life that are considered to be equally or more significant, in a clear process of withdrawal into the private sphere. Many observers have linked this tendency toward privatization to the gradual process of depoliticization in society. Finally, there is the idea that opposes the privatization/depoliticization hypothesis with one of a crisis in conventional politics and the concomitant

Spreading the word
Politics in the everyday life in the Basque Autonomous Community. Political posters and flyers adorn the walls of many public spaces, indicating that activism remains at a high level.
Photo: Iñaki Martínez de Albeniz.

expansion of a dual notion of the political: On the one hand, there is the extension of those spheres of social life susceptible to being considered political. It is not surprising, then, that one of the most recurring mottos of this new idea defends the notion that *everything is political.* And on the other, a political sociology has emerged that makes us more sensitive to this novel form of representing politics (or of politicizing reality).

BECAUSE the first model of articulating politics implies, in good part, a repeat of the processes and mechanisms that have already been addressed in the second part of the current work, I will concentrate here on the second and third models. These are based, respectively, on opposing (if not contradictory) hypotheses about depoliticization and new politicizations.

POLITICS ISN'T EVERYTHING

I will begin with the idea that, with the rise of a specialized professional politico-institutional sphere, the processes of social privatization in society call for only sporadic political participation in this "depoliticized" society. After Franco's death, the gradual creation of the so-called "state of the autonomies" brought into operation a new set of elements in Basque politics. These new elements substantially altered the framework of mechanisms that had favored the maintenance of the Basque nationalist code, a framework extensively explained in the second part of this book.

In the first place, political parties could be formed openly (see Section 1, Chapter 2 and Section 2, Chapter 11), the first consequence of which was the gradual breaking of a general anti-Franco unanimity and more specifically, that of the Basque nationalist world. Different political alternatives thus emerged and, mainly during elections, citizens had to choose from among these various options.

A second consequence of the new possibilities offered by these instruments of channeling political demands was, logically, a decrease in the political pressure exerted by society in general and, consequently, a change in social attitudes toward ETA's violence.

THIS SAID, the most striking change took place in what might be generically termed the way of understanding and experiencing politics. Privatization, brought with it the disappearance of the political from everyday life or the lifeworld of social actors and the appearance of alternative forms of producing meaning through activities far removed from politics, especially material consumption and individual careers. Disappearing as a totalizing center, politics became autonomous in the shape of a differentiated, specialized, and professional sphere in society. Once, a salvation ideology that (together with religion) had been shaped under a sacred shelter during the Franco years, politics now was secularized, and the it tone was ameliorated, in terms of both its communicative aspect in the public sphere and its qualitative, donorlike way of imparting individual or biographical meaning. Thus, politics lost its centrality as a strong socializing element and as a force unifying social life.

The withdrawal of politics from the realm of everyday life was, in good measure, a consequence of the recently emerged democratic institutions and political parties appropriating the public initiative. The political and social spheres differed from the point of view of their functionality and meaning. The new autonomy of the political sphere and its diffentiation from society via the processes of rationalization and institutionalization resulted in the defeat of centralized politics and its

Global, local, or both?
The public space in the Basque Autonomous Community in the era of global symbols. Tourists mingle at the entrance to the Guggenheim Museum, Bilbao. The Guggenheim, a global franchise museum, has increasingly come to represent Bilbao at an international level.
Photo: Iñaki Martínez de Albeniz.

---

attendant symbolism. Politics now became an affair of periodic electoral rituals in which the individual participates against the backdrop of a continuing political scenario that is "consumed" by citizens via the media (see Section 2, Chapter 8). The privatization process thus translates into a splitting of the public and the private: on the one side, a specialized public-political sphere emerges, and on the other, the private sphere gradually withdraws from the social. Once institutionalized, politics thus constitutes just one more sphere of reality next to the central nucleus of everyday life and must struggle with the others to form the backbone of an individual's social meaning. Politics ceases to be a totalizing and all-encompassing dimension, becoming just another option in the overall search for social meaning.

In sum, as a consequence of the institutionalization of politics, society underwent a privatization process that resulted in its depoliticization. Becoming autonomous, the strong (political) socializing functions that politics formerly possessed declined. The previously "politicized" network of social relations and socialization agents that sustained it (see Section 2, Chapters 5, 6, and 7) was reorganized, and its social presence and importance was reduced. For many observers, this loss of a political dimension within the intimate lives of the family, *cuadrilla*, and other enclaves of sociality, together with the gradual desertion of the streets as the public space of political expression, indicate the growing penetration of modern rationality in Basque society: Privatized Basque society escaped from the public light, stayed away from the streets, and took refuge in its homes, transforming them into spaces of security. Indeed, private life is above all a security mechanism. In a privatized society, the individual depends very much on his or her judgment and that of the family, acts on criteria based on private utility, and depends little on political beliefs and institutionalized communications.

EVERYTHING IS POLITICAL

THE ARGUMENT concerning the privatization and depoliticization of society is not the only one to address the process of political change during the last twenty-five years in the Basque Country. In fact it is, to a certain extent, reductionist. If it is indeed true that the advent of a differentiated political sphere brought with it a disaffection with politics on the part of society, it is equally true that such disaffection might also be understood as estrangement regarding a certain way of understanding and experiencing politics and specifically regarding professional politics as expressed in the triad formed by political parties, institutions, and the media. However, to assume a depoliticization of society in absolute terms, on the basis of an argument examined in the previous section, implies a certain insensitivity toward other forms of experiencing and understanding politics beyond mere party or institutional structuration. As the chapter on civil society and social movements in the second part of this book demonstrates, a new political culture is emerging outside the institutional channels of the Basque Country.

ONE SHOULD point out that the theoretical context of this new political culture is, without doubt, the redefinition to which the concepts of both politics (via postmodern thought and feminist political theory) and power (via Foucault's poststructuralism) have been subject. This is not the place to explore more thoroughly what I have termed this new political culture, but one should take note of its general meaning. Echoing the new understanding of politics that it promotes, we dedicate the following chapters of this book to examining new political and social identifications emerging in the Basque Country in light of a more complex political institutionalization than might appear at first, an institutionalization that, beyond its strengths (its political parties and institutions), enables, in the shadow of such institutions, the development of a phenomenon that is possible shed light on analytically only by extending one's sociological understanding—that is, through a sociology more sensitive to what has until recently received marginal consideration: weak and deterritorialized identities, the precarious, identity-based dimension of work, generational aesthetics and identity, gender identities, and so on.

Lesson thirteen

LEARNING OBJECTIVES

1. To understand the recent historical development of politics in general and of Basque nationalism in particular.
2. To study incidences of modern privatization processes of social life and the institutionalization or specialization of politics in the Basque Country.
3. To question the concept of the political by following the thread of political transformations in the Basque Country.
4. To analyze the spheres of social life that have been politicized during postmodernity.

REQUIRED READING

Daniele Conversi, *The Basques, the Catalans and Spain: Alternative Routes to Nationalist Mobilisation* (London: Hurst & Company, 1997).

Michael Keating, "The Minority Nations of Spain and European Integration: A New Framework for Autonomy," *Journal of Spanish Cultural Studies* 1, no. 1 (2000): 29–42.

SUGGESTED READING

Ulrich Beck, *The Reinvention of Politics: Rethinking Modernity in the Global Social Order* (Cambridge: Polity Press, 1997).

John R. Gibbins and Bo Reimer, *The Politics of Postmodernity: An Introduction to Contemporary Politics and Culture* (London: Sage, 1999).

WRITTEN LESSON FOR SUBMISSION

1. What did the passing of the Statute of Gernika in 1979 and the process of political institutionalization to which it led imply for Basque nationalism?
2. Do you think that the contemporary Basque Country is a depoliticized society?

Gabriel Gatti

14 · New identifications of Euskara

SUMMARY

Previously (Section 1, Chapter 4) we analyzed the historical importance of Euskara in relation to constructing a national identity in the Basque Country, together with its central role in the recent history of Basque nationalism. This chapter will demonstrate the role and place of the language in the most recent history of the Basque Country: the period of political institutionalization during which definitions of Basque identity have become more flexible and the boundaries between communities more open in such a way that subjects who were previously excluded from Basqueness for ethnocultural, political, linguistic, or social reasons can now call themselves Basques.

AFTER THE foundational stage of Basque nationalism, when race embodied the model subject and the boundaries between communities were closed, came another stage—the flowering of Basque nationalism, in which the most relevant feature became the linguistic and political community. In the period under study here, between the final years of the Franco regime and the initial period of institutionalization (1960–83), its most telling feature was the opening up and extending of the national community's limits: Both language and a commitment to the community conditioned the collective imaginary as regards who was or was not Basque.

This change was very significant, for during the era of foundational nationalism, when race was the main feature that objectified intercommunal differences, the incorporation of all those who were not previously pointed out as group members (a group that race delimited) lacked meaning socially. However, from the growth of Basque nationalism in the 1960s onward, it now became possible to consider integrating processes in a community whose main if not the only boundary was language: first as a way of joining, in a full, complete and exclusive way, a community interpreted as an aggregate with a moral and political nature, then, after political institutionalization, as a bond, precise, partial, and nonexclusive, to a community of citizens that became visible and was delimited by, among other things, possessing Euskara.

THE EXPANSION OF EUSKARA

IN THE 1960s, during the later years of the Franco regime and under the protective mantle of a thick and clandestine nationalist community, a powerful movement of linguistic recovery was born, out of which emerged a new imaginary, one that believed whoever learned the language could be incorporated into the community of Basques. New territories and new people thus began to join in the collective life of the Basque Country: geographical areas that sociogeographic representations of linguistic communities had previously labeled as either "Spanishized" or merely in terms of "contact" between the two communities (in other words, mixed). Agents that sociolinguistics located in non-Basque-speaking areas now nourished the linguistic community. Thus, the industrial, immigrant, urban, nontraditional world joined in the concept of Basqueness. Indeed, nobody could escape the changes brought about by these incorporations. Consequently, in the 1960s, the number of people studying Euskara grew, and with them the number of those who, from that time on, could call themselves Basque.

Extending Euskara
The Lizardi Euskaltegi, Bilbao. These special centers dedicated to the adult learning of Euskara are found throughout the towns and cities of the Basque Autonomous Community.
Photo: Iñaki Martínez de Albeniz.

THE PRESENCE of these new people and areas on the identity map of the Basque Country was strengthened in the 1980s by the process of political institutionalization. During this phase of politico-administrative stabilization of the national community, the way of viewing and understanding identity changed, and with it the form of viewing and understanding the language.

Because Basque identity was now managed from the institutions themselves, it no longer was the exclusive realm of the evaluative, symbolic, and associative framework of the national community. New social spaces inherited it, institutional spaces and individuals from the universe of citizenry—spaces and people that were not a priori the monopoly of any community.

One of the basic landmarks regarding Euskara in this institutionalization phase, one that had consequences not only for the language itself, but also as an indispensable source of information with which to approach it from a sociological perspective, was the establishment in 1981 of the Institute for the Teaching of Basque and Basque Language Literacy (HABE, Helduen Alfabetatze eta Berreuskalduntzerako Erakundea). HABE was established with the goal of creating an adequate infrastructure to face the needs of extending Basque to adults. Its creation led to a growing process of rationalization and professionalization of an initiative that, under the protection of Euskaltzaindia (the Academy of the Basque Language), had been created in 1967: The Coordination of Education and Literacy in Basque (AEK, Alfabetatze eta Euskalduntze Koordinakundea).

As a demonstration of the strength of Euskara's institutionalization, there were, on average through the 1980s and 1990s, 141 centers teaching Basque to adults, with fifty-five thousand students. In total, around two hundred and sixteen thousand people had attended a HABE or AEK center at least once by 1996, a not inconsiderable figure representing 30.4 percent of the non-Basque-speaking population of the Basque Autonomous Community.

THE CONSTRUCTION OF A NEW LINGUISTIC IMAGINARY

Sociologically analyzing, observing, and commenting on the society being analyzed, observed and commented on can also contribute to giving it shape: The categories of sociology can have an effect on reality and can, in some cases, transform it. They might even become a true source of social identification.

Speaking, as I am now, of new identifications surrounding Euskara, I cannot avoid demonstrating the importance this sociological interpretation of such new representations has had in their establishment. Effectively, the name by which those people who do not have Euskara as a mother tongue but learn it later—*euskaldunberris*—is, to a great extent, the product of sociological work.

SOCIOLOGY imagined categories that referred specifically to the sociological area between the Basque and Spanish-speaking communities ("contact areas" to refer to linguistically mixed geographical areas, where these two communities entered into contact with one another, and "quasi-Basque speakers" to denote those who occupied the diffuse linguistic area). Then it defined those who possessed that imprecise identity: *euskaldunberris*, neo-Basque speakers or neo-Basques.

Inventing this bridging category in the terrain of identities,[50] the social sciences contributed to the promotion of new identifications about Euskara, those emanating from people who approached the Basque language—and identity—to learn it. The effects were clear. Previously resistant frontiers separating the original linguistic communities—*erdaldunes* and *euskaldunes*, or Spanish speakers and Basque speakers—were now opened up. Processes of linguistic mobility and identity were socially facilitated between these communities. As Jacqueline Urla rightly points out, this has "open[ed] up

Selling Euskara
"Discover a New World. Euskara lets you discover Euskal Herria [the Basque Country]." Matriculation campaign by AEK (Alfabetatze eta Euskalduntze Koordinakundea, the Coordination of Education and Literacy in Basque) to encourage adults to learn Basque.
Illustration ccourtesy of AEK.

---

the possibility of envisioning ... movement across what are otherwise presented in the reports and in popular speech as mutually exclusive ethnolinguistic identities: Basque and non-Basque."[51] It became possible to think about a new identity-based rule: that of the *euskaldunberri* as an adherent to the community. Statistical categories became identification criteria, and the term "quasi-*euskaldun*" (originally a mere statistical addition) was transformed, through the *euskaldunberri* concept, into a name signifying identity.

NEW VALUES SURROUNDING EUSKARA

IN THIS WAY, the Basque community extended itself to agents who were, in principle, not especially close to Basque nationalism, and Euskara was transformed from an identity marker for a reduced number of agents into that of a much wider variety of people. Thus, from a scarce residual ethnic base of Basque nationalism, the terrain of Basqueness was significantly extended.

The Basque people's differential nature now did not depend on race. Being Basque was understood more flexibly and was more ambiguous.

BASQUENESS was no longer monolithic, but allowed various interpretations, some ethnic, others political, most of them cultural, some exclusive, others unknown, circumstantial, or partial. This was, to be sure, a powerful transformation. A politico-patriotic interpretation of identity and language belonging to the era associated with the growth of Basque nationalism, changed into one that, through the extension and administrative consolidation of its values, could be interpreted more in terms of opening up the boundaries of this community and its institutionalization, permitting entrance of agents until then far removed from it and the cultural legacy that distinguished it.

The Basque nationalist community thus became more accessible (in terms of its societal reach) than it had been up to that time as regarded Euskara and its categorizations. In other words, the somewhat circular nature of what had been understood in unitary fashion was broken. The national community had been understood as a system in which, without exact limits, the political, cultural, and territorial were joined as one. Now, with a more muted sense of unanimity within Basque nationalism, various ways of appreciating the language flourished that differed from previously dominant notions of the merely political or patriotic.

A process began that made it necessary to compare and legitimize new interpretations of identity and Euskara, even if only in a symbolic way. Since then, the language has become part of what has been termed the

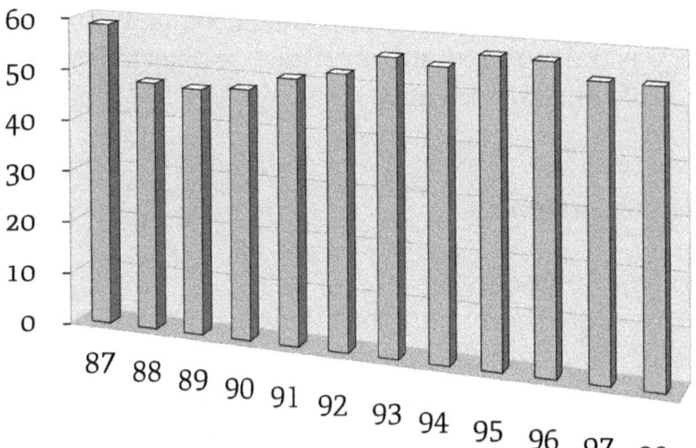

Table 27

1987–88	58,662	1993–94	56,261
1988–89	47,829	1994–95	55,172
1989–90	47,322	1995–96	57,835
1990–91	48,016	1996–97	57,531
1991–92	50,788	1997–98	54,569
1992–93	52,410	1998–99	54,497

Matriculation in Basque language learning centers for adults, 1986–99

These figures demonstrate a consistent level of people enrolled in Basque-language learning centers between the late 1980s and late 1990s. In fact, one-third of the non-Basque-speaking population of the Basque Autonomous community had attended such a center at least once by the mid-1990s.

Source: Author's calculation, based on data facilitated by HABE (www.habe.org).

"supermarket of meaning." Its nature as a differentiating instrument has become more general, liberating the previously rigid and now porous limits of the national community to transform it into a continent of multiple identifications. Like all other emblems of identity, Euskara was transformed into an attractive object for different "consumers of identity."

Lesson fourteen

LEARNING OBJECTIVES

1. To explore thoroughly the relationship between language and collective identity.
2. To assess the consequences that the political institutionalization process has had for Euskara.
3. To understand the close relationship between language and identity.
4. To question the importance of sociology for the construction of social life.

REQUIRED READING

Benjamín Tejerina, "Language and Basque Nationalism: Collective Identity, Social Conflict and Institutionalization," in *Nationalism and the Nation in the Iberian Peninsula: Competing and Conflicting Identities*, ed. Clare Mar-Molinero and Angel Smith (Oxford: Berg, 1996), 221–36.

Jacqueline Urla, "Being Basque, Speaking Basque: The Politics of Language and Identity in the Basque Country." PhD diss., University of California, Berkeley, 1987. (Ann Arbor, Mich.: UMI Dissertation Services, 1989).

SUGGESTED READING

Jacqueline Urla, "Cultural Politics in an Age of Statistics: Numbers, Nations and the Making of Basque Identity," *American Ethnologist* 20, no. 4 (1993): 818–43.

Gabriel Gatti, *Las modalidades débiles de la identidad* (Bilbao: UPV/EHU, 2002).

WRITTEN LESSON FOR SUBMISSION

1. How did the political institutionalization of Basque nationalism and other recent changes influence the change in values associated with Euskara and in the way in which Euskara shapes Basque identity?
2. Critically assess the role played by social science in constructing new representations of Euskara and identity.

Ignacio Irazuzta

15 · Generational and social change

SUMMARY

This chapter is concerned with the links between generational and social change in the Basque Country. Youth is examined as a social, rather than an essentialist construct. As such, it is susceptible to being expressed in various ways, along with other social categories. Special attention is paid to the changing relationships between youth, identity, and politics through a comparative analysis of two different moments in recent Basque history: the rise of ETA in the 1960s and the punk movement during the initial years of political institutionalization.

NORMALLY, we tend to think of the basic stages of life, such as childhood, youth, and adulthood, as parts of a universal experience that comes naturally to our condition as living beings and, therefore, as associated with the human biological cycle. This reasoning is fine, because, on the one hand, the experience of change across the span of a life is common to all cultures and, on the other, because such change is closely related to an alteration in our physical characteristics. Thus, one can differentiate between a child's and an adult's body in the same way as we can distinguish that of a woman from that of a man.

However, these issues that give our species an organic dimension, or the ways in which the basic life cycle is classified and the boundaries established between one stage and another (that is, between childhood and youth and between youth and adulthood), vary from culture to culture and one historical period to another. What today we generally think of as youth, the classification criteria of which continue to be vague, relative, and hardly objective, are a long way from those that prevailed in the Basque Country in the nineteenth century. Likewise, a young university student from Bilbao today has little in common with someone of a similar age in a Rio de Janeiro *favela*, or slum.

Although we all agree that such classifications are relative and vary culturally—or precisely because of this—social thought has still dedicated a lot of time to the subject. There has been a tendency to relate youth and social change to such an extent that, taking account of cultural standards and the behavior of youths, many people think it possible to predict a society's future. Without going into too much detail regarding the history of social thought and this subject, one might generally conclude that, beginning in the early twentieth century, social change began to be considered in terms of generational succession. Perhaps as a response to the European socialist movement, or also as a consequence of the development of a certain generational consciousness as the result of male losses during World War I, José Ortega y Gasset proposed the concept of generations as the engine of historical movement. Generations were thus set up as a substitute for social classes and as the guarantors of cultural change. Ortega y Gasset saw generational change as the most important concept in history and the hinge on which it moves. A similar importance has been afforded the concept by other observers (Karl Mannheim, for example), who moreover have related the notion of youth to marginality, that is, as a stage of life when one is not completely integrated into the social order.

HALFWAY through the 1940s, Talcott Parsons took up the issue once more from the scientific perspective of sociology and in light of an evident prolonging of the youth phase as a result of the generalized appearance of institutions of secondary education. The American

Activism through camaraderie
Group feeling survives among the younger Basque generations. A communal lunch organized by cuadrillas during Bilbao's annual fiesta. These groups often form the basis of social movements and combine friendship with grassroots activism.
Photo: Iñaki Martínez de Albeniz.

---

sociologist saw schools as boundaries, keeping youth out of the productive system and away from the relationships of social class. One could detect, then, the beginnings of a youth culture, different in a relative sense from adult cultural norms and characterized, with regard to Parsons's diagnosis about U.S. society at that time, by an irresponsible hedonism. In the United States, a teenage generation appeared whose cultural habits would subsequently be portrayed in many Hollywood movies. During the 1960s, sociological approaches to the subject, attentive to the trend of student revolts, also explored youth as the principal agent of change but, in this case, as the bearer of a counterculture, an alternative to what was already socially or culturally established.

SOCIOLOGICAL studies now examine the subject in relation to productive priority in contemporary societies and the twin crises of employment and extended school timetables, together with the gradual loss of rites of passage such as marriage and military service. In such a situation, most experts highlight the prolongation of the youth phase. Helena Wulff, for example, argues that "there has been some attention to the fact that the state of youth tends to last over an increasing number of years, partly due to the prolonging of schooling, partly due to unemployment. This can be understood in terms of a cultural moratorium, a period when young people are extending youth by ways of experimenting with different roles and thereby delaying adult responsibilities."[52]

However, this is not a uniform tendency—something common to all those who share the same age. For this reason, one usually speaks of youth as a "social construction," a term implying the relative, non-essentialist nature of the concept and therefore linked to diverse factors within the social process. One very important factor is the social structure. This allows one to distinguish sociologically, for example, between a young person employed in a fast-food company and another who is a student in a private university in Bilbao.

YOUTH AND ETHNICITY

Another factor in the construction of youth, especially in the Basque Country, is ethnicity. Ethnicity here, of course, refers to a dynamic process—linked to social and political processes associated with industrialization, urbanization, and political homogeneity produced by the national state—around which the similarities and differences between groups in a specific society are made. This dynamic process consists of imparting meanings to certain cultural, political, religious, and other elements that, on becoming attributes of social groups, make up the phenomenon of ethnic differentiation. This is, definitively, a question of an identification process in which people build up the meaning of their existence in relation to other people. In other words, it is a subjective experience of self-recognition that finds its objective aspect in recognition by others. Yet this phenomenon does not lack influence. Identity is reproduced from centers of symbolic production that endeavor to impose fixed symbols, shaping a certain unity out of the adaptation of different cultural characteristics to ethnic belonging.

REGARDING the dynamic nature of the ethnic identity phenomenon, numerous studies examine the topic of youth in the Basque Country.[53] As pointed out at the beginning of this chapter, one of the basic characteristics of the notion of youth links change to social reproduction—in short, to what can be termed "generational rupture" here. Taking account of these issues, what follows is an exploration of the most general dimensions concerning the subject of youth in the Basque Country.

THE GENERATION GAP IN BASQUE NATIONALISM

As a consequence of the long period of political prohibition associated with Franco's dictatorship in the Spanish state, a significant generational rupture took place in the Basque Country with the rise of ETA in the 1960s. This phenomenon might be interpreted, in this sense, as the result of a group of young Basques mixing anticolonial and Marxist ideas associated with 1960s left-wing ideology with those of Basque nationalism.

New spaces of youth socialization
Different premises are increasingly converted into meeting places for new generations of young people in the Basque Autonomous Community. Where once young people occupied outdoor public spaces, new generations now often seek more private, indoor meeting places. *Photo: Iñaki Martínez de Albeniz.*

As Alfonso Pérez-Agote has demonstrated, the rise of ETA in the 1960s revealed the most visible part of the generational rupture between the youth of that time and their parents' generation.[54] The rise of ETA implied a radicalization, both in terms of its interpretation of Basque nationalism and the incorporation of a left-wing Marxist ideology linked to a decolonization process that, in some cases, was close to positions that encouraged the use of an armed struggle to pursue political goals. The radicalized forms of political expression that took root in the violence of ETA against the state gained growing social support among the Basque people, thereby creating a certain novel public space of protest, given the political silence that characterized most of the Franco period.

THIS PROCESS of change within Basque nationalism, which, during the final years of the Franco regime, involved widespread sections of the Basque population (especially the youngest sectors), then underwent several transformations in the immediate aftermath of the authoritarian regime. This was especially the case with the process of institutional normalization that led to the creation of political parties and autonomous governments in the Spanish state. Political life started to flow into institutional channels and, concomitantly, the importance of the streets as a public space for political expression decreased. However, an important section of the populace continued to use radicalized forms of politics. The radical Basque nationalist Herri Batasuna (HB), although in the institutionalized form of a political party that gained a significant amount of support in the Basque Autonomous Community (16 percent of total votes) (see Section 2, Chapter 11), became a center of political attraction for younger generations. Moreover, it showed itself to be open to and an integrator of diverse forms of political and cultural expression among these new generations. Groups formed by ecologists, antimilitarists, sexual-orientation minorities, and feminists (among others) found in HB an encouraging and identifying space that helped, at the same time, to redefine and strengthen Basque nationalist symbolism. Moreover, this phenomenon coincided with an opposite tendency regarding youth participation among both Basque and Spanish constitutionalist political parties, that is, parties that wholly participated in the electoral game, filling positions in both central government and autonomous representative institutions.

THE REDEFINITION OF ETHNICITY

This type of political syncretism in the realm of radical Basque nationalism, or more specifically, in the so-called "world of HB," was not only a feature of youth political involvement. Cultural tendencies, as well, tendencies that involved other levels of social life, transcending the local boundaries of the Basque Country and that might not necessarily have had the political expression of membership, also came together within this framework. As the ethnographic work of Sharryn Kasmir demonstrates, in Mondragón (Gipuzkoa)—a highly industrialized, medium-sized urban area with a high number of immigrants from different parts of the Spanish state—punk culture among certain youth sectors intervened in the process of redefining Basqueness. The young sons and daughters of working-class immigrants found in punk a form of expression through which they could express their ethnic belonging. The attributes of Basqueness were thus renewed by substituting traditional diacritic indicators associated with ethnic nationalism (such as descent, or even the *txapela*, the traditional Basque beret) with cultural elements linked to punk culture, such as the biker jacket, body piercing, or the social condition of being unemployed. Another typical feature of these cases was the framing of social spaces, such as bars, that became meeting places of recognition for young unemployed people.

EVEN IF such a description might be equally valid for young people in the German, British, or American punk movements, in the case of the Basque Country, and especially in Mondragón, its special feature was the ethnic dimension, the way in which it gave access to Basqueness for young people deprived of its traditional attributes. One of the characteristics of the punk movement in general is that its members disregard political teleologies in constructing their identities, but in the local context mentioned above, this was not the case, because these were clearly expressed through their link to the radical Basque nationalist movement.

THIS CASE illustrates the relationships between the categories of youth, ethnicity, and identity in the Basque Country. It also highlights the central place the concept of youth occupies in explaining social change. Of course, this has not been a look at the entire experience of youth in the Basque Country. As was made clear from the outset, youth is a plural category that demonstrates its homogeneity only in statistical considerations of age groups in a specific society. Here I have examined a few aspects of this heterogeneous world in relation to the theme of identity. Without doubt, many other interesting questions could be raised: for example, concerning other new and prolific forms of youth associationism and its relation to the declining participation of this section of the population in traditional political institutions (see Section 2, Chapter 12). Whatever the case, the argument of this chapter has been to introduce some elements that might allow us to extend this analytical structure to other social and cultural contexts.

Lesson fifteen

LEARNING OBJECTIVES

1. To understand the dilemmas associated with defining a sociological concept of youth.
2. To identify the relative nature of the concept and link this to other categories such as identity and ethnicity.
3. To understand this issue in the context of the Basque Country.

4. To identify generational ruptures in the main periods defining the contemporary history of the Basque Country.

REQUIRED READING

Sharryn Kasmir, "'More Basque than You': Class, Youth and Identity in an Industrial Basque Town," *Identities: Global Studies in Culture and Power* 9 (2002): 39–68.

Helena Wulff, "Introducing Youth Culture in its Own Right: The State of the Art and New Possibilities," in *Youth Cultures: A Cross-Cultural Perspective*, ed. Vered Amit-Talai and Helena Wulff (London: Routledge, 1995), 1–18.

SUGGESTED READING

Eugenia Ramírez Goicoechea, *De jóvenes y sus identidades: Socioantropología de la etnicidad en Euskadi* (Madrid: CIS, 1991).

Alfonso Pérez-Agote, "The Future of Basque Identity," in *Basque Politics and Nationalism on the Eve of the Millennium*, ed. William A. Douglass, Carmelo Urza, Linda White, and Joseba Zulaika (Reno: Basque Studies Program, 1999), 54–67.

WRITTEN LESSON FOR SUBMISSION

1. Critically describe the relationship between youth and ethnicity in the Basque Country.
2. Point out and comment on those elements that make up the relationship between politics and young people in the Basque Country.

Elsa Santamaría

16 · Identity: the new perspective of labor

SUMMARY

This chapter first examines the changes taking place in the socioeconomic structure of the Basque Country and how a new labor panorama is emerging out of an economic restructuring during the last twenty-five years, both at a local and a global level. Then, taking account of such changes, this chapter is concerned with questioning the industrial, salaried work model as insufficient in explaining the complex reality of labor in contemporary societies and with the role of new representations of work in constructing social reality.

THE CURRENT notion of work is a product of diverse explorations into the nature of the world, society, and the individual in the major currents of thought throughout history. Work has not always meant what it represents and designates today. Like any social phenomenon, it always responds to a contextual reality that both conditions and legitimizes it, and through a foundation in this definition of reality, it becomes socially meaningful. There is little doubt that presently, the dominant work model is that of salaried employment.

This model is the product of a historical development in which one can differentiate three stages: In the eighteenth century, people began to recognize the position of work in society as an instrument of creating wealth and therefore as a potentially emancipating factor for the individual. Work thus became associated with individual contributions to society, as an object of exchange in the market that could be negotiated through a contract, helping the individual to integrate into the social whole and shaping social relations.

It wasn't until the nineteenth century that work was seen as a transforming factor of both the individual and the world. Work could humanize the world and even transform humans themselves. It was at that time that people began to establish an ideology of work in which it appeared as an expression of real creative liberation and as an instrument of a true collective identity that was, however, impeded by the precarious working conditions and alienation suffered by workers themselves. Karl Marx, the main ideologue of this notion of work, believed that production and work form the central basis of social ties. This argument, which later had an important effect on the development of socialist and even classic liberal thought, was consistent with his notion of work: that it was no longer a creative, liberating agent and that it would become the basic vital necessity only when one could freely produce—that is, when the salary system had been abolished. In this way, work would no longer represent effort, sacrifice, and suffering, but instead the fullness of one's self, the full potential of humanity, and the living expression of societies.

WITH THE progress of time and the eroding of Marxist ideas, social-democratic thought and the development of the capitalist system transformed the salaried relationship into the basis of the social contract. The salary now was seen as the channel through which wealth flows, allowing one to achieve personal fulfillment and a fairer social order, mainly through rising wages and consumerist possibilities. This model of salaried work, which still prevails, is tied to a specific type of work—employment—that, situated in the public and mainly male sphere, has become the symbolic center of society. Thus, the practice of work became *the* principal condition of belonging to society, given that it not only grants the individual social benefits, well-being, and security,

The work ethic hewn in stone
The original sign for apprentice training at the Vocational School of Mondragón, Gipuzkoa. Founded by José María Arizmendiarrieta, this subsequenbtly became the Mondragon Cooperative Corporation, today one of the biggest employers in the Basque Autonomous Community.
Photo: Iñaki Martínez de Albeniz.

---

but generates social cohesion, regulating both personal and social identity.

THE CONCEPT of work, then, has been the result of a specific sociohistorical evolution. It hasn't always been associated with ideas implying the creation of value, the transformation of nature, and personal achievement, however much these ideas still resonate today. It's a stratified object, not only because it has multiple meanings (as a productive factor, a creative means of freedom,

---

a means of distributing revenue, the assigner of one's socioeconomic position, and the means of access to social rights for each individual), but also because it's understood by means of a mixture of theoretical questions and approaches concerning how to understand how the world, society, an individuals themselves function.

THE CENTRALITY OF WORK IN SOCIETY

Employment, the concept of work inherited from modernity, responds to an identity-based feeling that also stems from modernity. Work exists at the center of social life and becomes a constitutive element of identity. In the modern project, identity is generally understood as a stable entity or an inhabitable place for subjects where they are recognized as such by themselves and others. In other words, work is regarded as a shaper of identity in space-time, providing coherence and stability in developing personal biographies.

This notion of identity has been sustained by a means of academic knowledge produced in the realm of human sciences, based on the model of the modern Cartesian subject, which sees the individual as rational and transcendent. As such, with a certain degree of stability and progress in one's professional career and a more or less normal and predictable sense of time, subjects can construct their life projects in a long-term way, shaping their lives on the basis of their work. It only remains to say that this notion is more properly understood as a Western, male model with enormous faith in the idea of the evolution and progress of societies.

BROADLY speaking, from a macro point of view, work can articulate the social order and perform its integration, whereas from a micro point of view, it shapes the meaning of life and the social aspect of identity. Individuals work in and for society, and it is through their work that they manage to be recognized, as well as to feel socially useful and integrated. Moreover work provides one with social status, at both an individual and a family level. Work, in sum, is the basis of social bonds, and not only because it is one of the principal channels of socialization and social integration, but also because it constitutes the pillar around which individuals are identifiable in their everyday lives and where they make contact with other people within the same boundaries. One might, thus, advocate a fixed image, instituted and centered on the sphere of work, in which workers are literally "nicely placed" in their jobs.

HOWEVER, one must also take into account that in our societies, not just any social or economic activity is considered as employment in a strict sense. Employment is an economic activity that requires knowledge, ability, and experience and constitutes a means of earning sufficient social support, thereby becoming the foremost activity in life, the main occupation of one's time, conceived of as an inescapable daily duty that confers social meaning.

However, it is no less true that the categories of both employment and employee also reveal a dialectic opposite: unemployment and the unemployed. As opposed to the above definition, the unemployed person is "misplaced," or someone who, through not having a job, cannot receive a salary. Such a person thus has a reduced personal income and is of no use (in the sense of being productive) to society. Furthermore, such people lack a key reference point from which to shape their identities, as well as their social capital in terms of status and social relations.

What I have examined up to this point might be understood in terms of a center-periphery logic: The more

Free time in Basque society
The other face of work, or the free time afforded by work. Bathers on the Gros beach in Donostia–San Sebastián, Gipuzkoa, reflected in a window of the Kursaal Auditorium and Conference Center.
Photo: Fernando Elkoroiribe.

---

someone's work takes the form of employment, the more one is at the center of society. This social center of our communities is thus formed essentially by professional adult males, and those people who don't reach this center or are expelled from it, mainly the unemployed, remain on the periphery.

WORK ISN'T found only where it is institutionally defined, however, for it also exists in the interstices of this central system. It is from this perspective that today one might begin to comprehend the infinite number of situations in which people travel through the labor market, whether on its margins or outside it, both in voluntary form and obliged to by circumstances. We can now see the transformations that allow us to visualize more clearly the institutional part of the contemporary work world.

NEW IDENTIFICATIONS ABOUT LABOR IN THE BASQUE COUNTRY

In recent decades, the sphere of labor has undergone multiple processes of change. There has, in particular, been a demonstrable heterogeneous trend, a tendency to make things more complex, and greater fragmentation, not only in the forms that work takes, but also in the functions and meaning of the term itself.

SCHEMATICALLY, one might sum up all this by saying that the former salaried, industrial, manual, disciplined, and standardized society has given way to a new tertiary, informational, flexible, and less regulated society. The closing down of (mainly industrial) economic sectors such as the iron and steel industry has led to an expansion in service activities in the tertiary economic sector, such as information technology, health and social work, commercial activity, tourism, and so on that have undergone an unprecedented growth. A perfect example of this tendency is the case of Greater Bilbao, formed by the city itself plus thirty-four neighboring municipalities. During the last quarter of the twentieth century, this region was considered an industrial area par excellence, thanks to the development of primary and secondary economic sectors, including mining, the iron and steel industry, and the rise of an important banking sector (see Section 1, Chapter 1). However, all that remains of this past today can only be found in museums, conference centers, and other places related mainly to the spheres of culture, tourism, and leisure time.

Yet this emphasis on the tertiary sector implies a significant change not just as regards defining the division of labor, but also (and mainly) in terms of both collective and individual identities characteristic of the process of industrialization. These changes led to the loss of a certain collective outlook in experiencing one's leisure time, doing things, and giving life meaning, and this crisis of identity first affected people that had for generations been miners, factory workers, and shipbuilders. During the 1980s and 1990s, they went through the harsh experience of unemployment, early retirement, industrial downsizing, and, generally speaking, a more precarious life. In fact, the highest ever recorded unemployment levels in the Basque Country date from the period between 1985 and 1995, when they reached 24 percent.[55]

GIVEN THAT unemployment levels have dropped in recent years, to around 8.4 percent in 2003, for example, job redundancy is no longer a serious problem. Indeed, now the principal issue that concerns people is the type of jobs that are being created. Conventional work forms based on full-time jobs, clearly defined occupational tasks, and a professional career model for the rest of one's life are already things of the past. Work is now characterized by its flexibility. People speak about flexible salaries, schedules, contracts, and even personal flexibility. Nowadays, a person must be willing to change jobs and experience numerous different work situations, something that makes it tremendously difficult to plan life-long projects.[56] Individuals move about from one situation to another much faster than before, and the formerly solid structure of industrial society has given way to a variety of fragmented experiences that lead to other kinds of divisions and inequalities. Elsewhere, new legal and social forms of contracting workers and self-employment have proliferated. Now there are new types of agreements—such as end-of-work, semicontrolled, and work-experience contracts, as well as internships—and other organizational experiences, among which I would highlight worker cooperatives.[57]

YOUNG PEOPLE, whether obliged to or voluntarily, delay their entry into the workplace or work at its margins and, elsewhere, their elders are also beginning to accept early retirement, thereby affecting a large part of the productive sector, although this has been the case mainly in the industrial sphere. Both movements lead to a shortening of the years that people dedicate to taking part in the workplace. At the same time, fixed, indefinite work contracts have become scarcer in the face of the more dominant temporary contracts, end-of-work contracts, internships, and so on. This might lead, among other things, to less actual work time and greater labor instability. And finally, the work schedule has also been affected by the general tendency toward reduced working hours, with part-time work now increasingly taking the place of full-time employment. The proliferation of part-time work is significant, especially among women: For example, 36 percent of all jobs obtained by women in the second third of 2003 in the Basque Country were based on temporary, part-time contracts, compared with 14 percent for men.[58] As regards this tendency, one should also point out that the reduced working day lives side-by-side with its opposite: in some cases, a working day extends to outrageous limits. The latter tendency is typically the case for young people, immigrants, and those people who, one might say, have become addicted to work.

The precarious nature of employment today is a theme running through the sphere of labor. As a result of this precarious situation in the forms and conditions of employment, a gap has emerged in the way in which people experience work, mainly between those who have stable, well-paid positions and an increasing number of people who suffer the consequences of having to be more flexible in their work, as well as of having to experience the volatility and unreliability of contemporary jobs.

Lesson sixteen

LEARNING OBJECTIVES

1. To reflect on historical notions about the idea of work and the process by which it is socially constructed.
2. To analyze the principal transformations in the representation and meaning of work in society and sociology.
3. To trace a general overview of employment and work in the Basque Autonomous Community.
4. To analyze the development of employment and transformations in work from the point of view of their meaning and new identities brought into play.

REQUIRED READING

Manuel Castells, *The Information Age: Economy, Society, and Culture*, vol. 1, *The Rise of the Network Society* (Malden, Mass.: Blackwell, 1996), 201–79.

Richard Sennett, *The Corrosion of Character: The Personal Consequences of Work in the New Capitalism* (New York: W. W. Norton, 1998).

SUGGESTED READING

Dominique Méda, *El trabajo: Un valor en peligro de extinción* (Barcelona: Gedisa, 1998).

Amparo Serrano, "Representación del trabajo y socialización laboral," *Sociología del trabajo* 33 (1998): 27–49.

WRITTEN LESSON FOR SUBMISSION

1. Explain why work is such a central part of the social structure and an important element of integration in contemporary societies.
2. Evaluate the changes taking place in the Basque labor market and critically interpret the new meanings of experiencing work for subjects.

Beatriz Cavia

17 · Gender identities

SUMMARY

This chapter will examine gender as one of the basic areas attracting new identifications. I will focus on the social and sociological production of gender at different levels: from gender relations seen in terms of their institutionalization as a focus of study for Basque social sciences to the political dimension of gender as channeled through feminism and nationalism, as well as through institutionalized gender politics. Finally, to evaluate the social and identity-based dimension of gender, I will look at an especially relevant ritual for sociology: the alardes, military-style parades at the center of two local annual festivals in Hondarribia and Irún (Gipuzkoa).

THE NOTION of gender identity rests on a symbolic construction of the biological notion of sex in a dichotomy between masculinity and femininity. However, this apparent distinction between sex and gender becomes more complicated if one scrutinizes the modern process of constructing the categories of sexuality and identity. Not even traditional representations of gender identity are free of the pressure of change, and indeed are also confronted by questions of hybridization between sex and gender or masculinity and femininity. I take gender to be a threefold condition: as a performative process that acquires meaning through the display and representation of sexual identity, as a social category of identification, and as an analytical category for the social sciences.

From the basis of these assumptions I will demonstrate the most relevant changes in the symbolic and material construction of gender in contemporary Basque society and sociology. First I will focus on the issues that the study of gender has provoked in the social sciences since its institutionalization as a specific discipline of study and object of research. Then I will take account of social changes that have taken place in gender relations and the forms of expressing, representing, and understanding gender identity in Basque society. Next, I will try to gauge the political dimension of gender identity as channeled through feminism (as a social movement) and institutionalized gender politics. Finally, I will illustrate the conjunction of contested constructions of gender and Basque nationalism by reference to issues that have been raised about the *alardes* of Hondarribia and Irún.

THE INSTITUTIONALIZATION OF GENDER AS A SOCIOLOGICAL AND SOCIAL CATEGORY

IN THE 1980s, gender studies gradually became more important in the social sciences addressing Basque topics. A landmark in this regard was the creation of the Interdisciplinary Seminar on Women's Studies at the Anthropology Laboratory in the Philosophy and Education Sciences Faculty of the University of the Basque Country in 1981. Thereafter, the publication in 1985 of *Mujer y realidad vasca* (The Basque woman and reality)—compiled by Teresa del Valle and made up of diverse studies of women in rural, coastal, and urban areas—and in 1987 of *La mujer y la palabra* (Women and speech) marked the beginning of an extensive bibliography on gender and feminism that became more and more diversified through the 1990s. At that time, gender studies started to grow significantly, with numerous research projects and publications that opened up the subject matter and highlighted the complexity of the issues.

These diverse studies focused on aspects related to power and authority, space-time coordinates, urban questions, artistic and scientific production, the representation and construction of corporeality, health and maternity, nationalism, feminism, sexuality, and peripheral forms of gender identities. These are important approaches that explore the logic of power in all its dimensions and question the traditional institution of gender and its associated themes of family, the distinction between the public and the private spheres, and the body and identity.

At an institutional level, the creation of the Basque Women's Institute (Emakunde) allowed for the increased visibility of specific gender issues and of work in certain social sectors, beginning with advocating the application of policies of equality. To do this, it was necessary to provide a diagnosis of the situation of women in the Basque Country and their institutional needs.

GENDER STUDIES in the Basque Country don't just involve studies about women, but have been expanded to encompass the notion of gender identity as a process by which both masculinity and femininity are represented and exercised, thereby including developments linked to the material nature of gender and sexuality and the construction of masculinities and diverse forms of identity. Within this context, there are more and more studies of gay, lesbian, transsexual, and transgender identities. I will now address the most relevant changes highlighted by such studies.

SOCIAL CHANGE IN CONTEMPORARY GENDER REPRESENTATIONS

In general terms, the position of women has been transformed, mainly as a result of their incorporation into the labor market and changes in the traditional family, as

Changing times
Democracy, even in one's sexual preferences. A poster advocating equality for homosexuals by the Basque organization of gays and lesbians, Gehitu.
Photo: Gehitu.

---

well as their inclusion (minimal, but developing) in academia and politics. Another fundamental change has taken place in the separation between reproduction and sexuality, and this in turn has influenced a transformation in perceptions of the body, couple relations, and maternity, aspects that, until the Franco generation, constituted the central pillar of expressing and defining women's identity.

THESE CHANGES came as a result of transformations in the socialization process, a key practice in the creation and consolidation of gender identities, and in the way of understanding corporeality, femininity, and relations between genders. One should, however, recognize the difficult modification of a socialization that reproduces role distinctions according to sex and that naturalizes difference, even if it has suffered changes in ways of understanding, assuming power, and withholding its capacity for action in the social sphere. The transformation processes of recent decades are the product of activity on the part of feminisms and their inclusion in social sciences, in a fashion similar to the transformations and the crisis in traditional Basque institutions.

Finally one should point out that, from this dual interaction, the category "women"—as a subject of feminisms and an object of study—has been displaced by a concept of gender in which other related and identity-based dimensions come together and whose definition doesn't exactly fit its biological counterpart of sex.

FEMINISM, NATIONALISM, AND MATRIARCHY

I have already stated above that feminism, as a social movement, led to important changes in terms of redefining contemporary notions of gender. Feminist demands, based on different ideological forms and practices of resistance, encouraged new ways of understanding femininity. Feminist movements have evolved in the last thirty years into what might be termed the "third wave," giving rise to a diverse number of perceptions and ways of understanding identity and widely contributing to a redefinition of sociological and social categories of gender.

IN THE Basque context, feminism has been very important politically. With the influence of social sciences and the changes that have taken place in the social structure since the end of the Franco dictatorship, a whole new panorama has opened up, both for women and for subcultures based on gender and sex, leading to new spaces of visibility and expression. In this regard, one must address the significance of gay, lesbian, and transsexual movements. In recent years, these movements have acquired more and more importance in representations of sexuality. Here one should note how the institution of gender, polarized between masculinity and femininity, acquires an ample spectrum of possibilities through these new movements and their study on the part of academia.

GENDER ALSO became a category of analysis regarding nationalism, first, because (together with nationalism) it forms part of a wider construction of identity and the shifting meaning of being Basque; and second, because both themes participated in essentializing identity (national, masculine and feminine).

Both gender and nationalist constructions of identity overlap in social-scientific studies, but they are also related to the meaning and the specific evolution of certain feminisms, as well as to the ideological and political specificity in the Basque context. Feminism and nationalism, for example, find common ground in the idea of Basque matriarchy as a symbol in which the woman appears as the solid base of tradition and identity.

The first gender studies appeared with the specific and critical vocation of demythologizing matriarchy, a cultural construct on which a great deal of traditional images of women was based. Their purpose was to deconstruct anthropologically this myth from feminist positions rooted in a new academic and social context related to a change of subjectivities and declarations about gender.

Matriarchy is the symbolic construction that gives women a role as transmitters of cultural values and language within the institution of the family, assigning them a centrality as pillars of the family and tradition.

Transformations in Marriage Patterns
After 1975 marriage rates in Basque society gradually declined. At the same time, there was a growth in the mean age at marriage, as well as both civil (as opposed to church) and second marriages.
Photo: PhotoDisc, Inc.

This image confers authority on women in the private sphere and mythologizes their function as mothers and wives. Thus, their role is relegated to the domestic realm, taking as given the distinction between public and private spheres, the social differentiation of roles, and socialization according to gender.

Based on this hypothesis of differentiating socialization, the first significant studies of gender began to appear in the 1980s. At present, research that critically addresses this cultural construction and analyses of such topics as the mythical witch Mari seek a complex rereading of Basque gender and identity.

THE *ALARDES*

We have seen the overlapping of nationalism, feminism, and the figure of matriarchy and how these links are obvious in studies of gender relevant to the Basque context, as well as how they influence and assign specificity to the topic itself. Now we'll examine one specific case where these mutual influences are reflected: that of a Basque ritual in the border towns of Irún and Hondarribia in Gipuzkoa: the *alardes*.

The *alardes* are military-style parades that recall the historical existence of municipal militias. These festivals extol local identity and territorial resistance that was carried out militarily in these frontier towns centuries ago. In the reproduction of these rituals, one element alone has remained steadfast: the ban on women participating as soldiers—exclusively relegating their participation to the role of serving girls—while many other traditional aspects (such as the flags that decorate people's balconies and the exclusive participation of people from the towns themselves) have been changed without provoking any conflict.

THE DEMAND by women to be able to participate as soldiers, leading to a heated debate in recent years, is an attempt to occupy masculinity symbolically in the parade. And the resistance this has provoked among so-called "traditionalist" sectors has resulted in a significant degree of social conflict, revealing the imbalances produced by social change as well as different ways of understanding collective identities. Here, the positions of different agents give us some idea about how this problem originally derived from a split between those in favor of the traditional festival and those supporting a mixed *alarde*, a split that has affected both Basque institutions and public opinion.

RESISTANCE to change implies (among its adherents) the reproduction and preservation of the patriarchal system and of the traditional view of the Basque woman as a wife, mother and reproducer, of the family, without taking account of the fact that in the contemporary social realm, a number of changes have taken place in the order of gender relations. Moreover, the traditional role of women to which this appeals is that of a family anchor or objectified subject (such as in the role of serving girl).

This is an extremely complex issue that should not just be interpreted as a case of gender discrimination, given that it is related to the more complex matter of identity (both national and gender), as well as to a crisis in certain institutions linked to the border location of these towns. In other words, this reveals a crisis of collective border identity, a crisis of industrial society, a crisis resulting from the postindustrial situation, with its growth in services that require the free movement of goods and people, and ultimately, a crisis of masculinity. This should be analyzed from these multiple dimensions. It also reveals signs of a how contemporary Basque identity is being constructed. It highlights a representation of gender as an analytical category from which one can address contemporary processes and as a solid symbolic category for producing all things social.

CONCLUSION

One might sum up the changes in the sociological and social representation of gender through the following characteristics. During the last thirty years in the Basque Country, there has been a consolidation of gender studies in Basque academia. Gender has been transformed into an analytical category from which one can address contemporary forms of identity, while at the same time it has shaped important changes in Basque society. Feminism, nationalism, and sociological research thus are intimately connected in the social construction of gender identities in the Basque Country. The emergence of new forms of expressing and of representing gender is a response to the transformations and crises of traditional institutions and an example of new ways of constructing meaning. New gender identities question stable concepts and representations of masculinity and femininity, leaving room for an interpretation of partial or fragmented identity that can be shaped, consumed, and transformed. The *alardes* of Irún and Hondarribia allow one to present a gender-based analysis of a complex perspective on the different dimensions that come together in the social construction of identity in Basque society.

Lesson seventeen

LEARNING OBJECTIVES

1. To understand a general overview of gender in social science and contemporary Basque society.
2. To analyze the concept of gender and its theoretical implications.
3. To trace the links between different dimensions of contemporary Basque identity as regards gender.
4. To analyze specific cultural phenomena such as the *alardes* of Irún and Hondarribia from a multidimensional perspective of gender and identity.

REQUIRED READING

Margaret Bullen, "Gender and Identity in the *Alardes* of Two Basque Towns," in *Basque Cultural Studies*, ed. William A. Douglass, Carmelo Urza, Linda White, and Joseba Zulaika (Reno: Basque Studies Program, 1999), 149–77.

Mari Luz Esteban, "Embodied Anthropology: Anthropology from Oneself," in "Medical Anthropology and Anthropology," special issue, *AM-Revista della Società Italiana di Antropologia Medica* 11–12 (2001): 173–89.

SUGGESTED READING

Teresa Del Valle, *Modelos emergentes en los sistemas y las relaciones de género* (Barcelona: Narcea, 2002).

Carmen Díez Mintegi, "Sistemas de género, desigualdad e identidad nacional," in *Sociedad vasca y construcción nacional: Retos y perspectivas teóricas y sociales*, ed. Pedro Albite et al. (Donostia: Gakoa, 1999). 147–74.

WRITTEN LESSON FOR SUBMISSION

1. Critically consider the relations between feminisms, academia, and processes of constructing contemporary Basque gender identities.
2. Analyze the different dimensions that have intervened in the social conflict emerging out of the *alardes*.

Ignacio Irazuzta

18 · The Basque diaspora

Globalization and identity

SUMMARY

The concept of a diaspora is one of the most important examples of identity in today's postmodern world, where the nation-state has lost much of its centrality and power. This chapter explores the varied realities grounding the concept, from its traditional definition as the traumatic exodus of a people to its embrace of contemporary social phenomena such as economic migration, political exile, transnational workers, and traditional migratory ethnic communities, all phenomena of which Basques are good examples. It also analyzes the steps taken to institutionalize the Basque diaspora and thereby to embrace the challenge of identity that it poses.

MANUEL Castells has repeatedly highlighted the argument that the spectacular changes taking place in the new millennium point to a bipolar tendency in contemporary society.[59] On the one hand, one can clearly see the emergence of instrumental-reason-based global exchange networks operating mainly through the use of new technologies, and on the other, a similarly evident tendency toward the emergence of an existentially based sense of self. This is a simultaneous dual process that favors a schizophrenic arrangement between function and meaning in our societies. We are thus witnessing a process that appears to be redefining our political institutions and spaces, as well as assigning culture a new place, a process that, ultimately, is having a number of new social effects.

One sign of the novel quality of this general trend concerns the notion of diaspora in social science. In specific contexts, for example, the more traditional term

Common bonds
The Monument to the Basque Sheepherder by the sculptor, Nestór Basterretxea, on the road up to the Shrine of Arantzazu, Gipuzkoa. It evokes the same sculptor's "Bakardade" (Solitude), a monument in honor of Basque sheepherders, inaugurated in 1989 in Rancho San Rafael, Reno, Nevada.
Photo: Iñaki Martínez de Albeniz.

"immigration" has now been replaced by "diaspora." Yet this doesn't mean that academia has suddenly discovered the phenomenon of people moving all over the world. Quite the contrary, in fact, because for some time, this phenomenon has defined an anthropological characteristic of human beings in general. What appears to be specific to diasporas is that, at least in the most simple and deductive definition, they refer to the dispersion of a people from their homeland.[60] This definition has traditionally served to characterize the experience of various peoples, such as Jews and Armenians. However, the term is increasingly being employed in a wider sense, beyond its original meaning of a traumatic exodus, to encompass more modern social phenomena, including identity-based groups and expressions such as immigrants, refugees, transnational workers, exiles, and traditional migratory ethnic communities.[61]

IN THE CONTEXT of a growth in communications and transport, these situations reveal the increasingly apparent face of a global-scale economy and its concomitant expression in the gestation of new centers and peripheries, marked out by areas of either advanced economic development or poverty. Nor should one discount the influence of political upheavals in nation-states on the emergence of diasporic communities, given that such events are among the main reasons behind the problem of exiles and refugees. Taking all these phenomena into account, one might come to the following somewhat paradoxical conclusion: that, while fewer and fewer people live in the land of their ancestors, the ethnic aspects of referring to one's place of origin and ancestors are increasingly coming to define the collective identities of such groups. This is a social process that, as some observers have suggested, imparts a tribal nature on diaspora identities.[62]

Among specialists on this topic—which, to be sure, is becoming more and more popular in social sciences and leading to multidisciplinary theoretical and methodological perspectives—some observers have attempted to list a series of characteristics defining this transnational collective experience. Among these, one might highlight the following. The group establishes itself outside its original homeland in at least two peripheral places away from this original center. They maintain a memory or myth associated with their place of origin. A belief runs through the group of not being fully accepted in the host society. They believe they will eventually return to their place of origin one day and, thus, they will try and maintain or reestablish their original homeland. Among the group's attributes there also is a sentimental recourse to feeling a sense of connection to their homeland.[63]

SOME OF these characteristics point to aspects that, following Kim Butler, should be explained in more detail. For example, one might consider the idea of a dispersal in at least two different places from the original homeland as a precondition for forging links between diaspora groups originating in the same place. It is exactly this dispersion that points to the novel quality of the phenomenon.[64] In this aspect concerning the construction and reproduction of ties around the place of origin, it is important that there is either a real or imagined relationship with the homeland. Although one-third of the characteristics listed above might be debatable, to some extent at least (I will elaborate on this below), the list highlights the conditions for developing a certain consciousness of ethnic belonging that differentiates the group as a minority from the wider society in which it lives. The fact that one can speak about a diaspora from the existence of at least two generations helps to corroborate the last two characteristics. Diasporas are, in this sense, multigenerational, that is, they combine the individual experiences of immigration with a collective history of dispersion and communal regeneration outside the place of origin.

Given the fact that diasporas are multiple and therefore entail diverse experiences, we often find cases in which none of the above features appear and other characteristics emerge. This demonstrates the richness of the subject and the dynamic, constantly unstable nature of the processes by which ethnicity is being redefined. One might agree with James Clifford that the term "diaspora" involves not just transnational ideas, but also political struggles to define the local sphere as a distinctive community in various historical contexts of displacement. It is, in sum, a question of new bonds and tensions that are emerging out of the growing flow of transnational capital and communications, something that is often termed "globalization." In what follows, I will try and highlight some elements of this general process, demonstrating the particularities of the so-called "Basque diaspora."

THE BASQUE DIASPORA: HISTORICAL ANTECEDENTS

BASQUE history is a tale of migration that, one might contend, began with the colonization of the Americas from the fifteenth century onward. That said, the greatest migrations, in both Basque and European terms, actually took place in the nineteenth and early twentieth centuries. This was a long period of migration, caused principally by the transformation of a rural to an industrial society, a transformation that, in the case of the Basque Country, was related to both the nineteenth-century Carlist wars and the twentieth-century Spanish Civil War. This Basque migratory flow spread all over the world, with communities established in Australia, New Zealand, South Africa, Canada, the United States, and most of the countries in South and Central America, as well as in most of the principal European and Spanish cities, such as Paris, London, Barcelona, and Madrid. From that time, and up until the present day, throughout the above-mentioned places, *euskal etxeak*, or Basque centers, have tried to reproduce ties of ethnic belonging among their members. These people tend both to maintain some kind of relationship with the homeland and to assign an identity through which they can negotiate integration into their host societies.

The specific nature of the Basque case, its lack of a nation-state, has meant that, in part, one of the strongest expressions of ethnic nationalism in Europe has emerged (at least in that part of the Basque Country in the Spanish state) and also that (as a consequence of this) the territory claimed by this nationalism is under the political authority of two nation-states: the so-called Iparralde (the North Basque Country) in the French state, and Hegoalde (the South Basque Country), composed of the provinces of Araba, Gipuzkoa, and Bizkaia in the Basque Autonomous Community (see Section 1, Chapter 2), together with the Foral Community of Navarre in the Spanish state. This complex relationship, tied to the demand for ethnic belonging in different political spaces, is also a feature of meeting places and their respective identities outside the Basque Country. Thus, one finds French Basque, Navarrese, or simply Basque centers throughout the world's Basque communities.

A SIGNIFICANT change in the life of these centers came with the influx, in the 1940s and 1950s, of exiles from the Spanish Civil War. With their arrival, the existing Basque migrant communities experienced a form of regeneration that led to an increasing sense of diaspora in the various countries of the Americas, although this was only a feature of what was previously the Spanish Basque community. During and after the Spanish Civil War, there was a concerted effort, among Basque collectivities in the Americas, either to reestablish a sense of solidarity or to create one from scratch. This new impulse might be dated from the creation of the Basque government-in-exile during the 1930s and especially be attributed to the activity of the *lehendakari*,

Transatlantic Basque Identity
Evidence of aesthetic crossover in the Basque diaspora. The entrance to a country residence in Córdoba, Argentina, where, flanked by two neoclassical gilded lions, one can read the words "Gure Etxea" (Our House, in Euskara).
Photo: Fernando Elkoroiribe.

---

or president, José Antonio Aguirre, together with other exiles in Argentina, Mexico, and Venezuela, because they negotiated with local governments a means by which other Basques forced into exile could swiftly and relatively easily settle in these countries.[65] The activity of these exiles also furthered the reproduction for Basque nationalism, because this form of immigration included many nationalist intellectuals, and they formed different bodies to extend Basque culture, which in turn contributed to reproducing ethnic consciousness. Publishing houses and newspapers reproducing this Basque nationalist imaginary were especially prolific in Argentina, together with others in Uruguay and Mexico. Another significant event was the World Basque Congress, held in Paris in 1956 under the auspices of diaspora Basques. Basque intellectuals, politicians, and artists from all over the world met, reinforcing their ethnicity under the framework of consecrating Basque culture.

THE INSTITUTIONALIZATION OF THE BASQUE DIASPORA

Another key event for the Basque diaspora, in the sense that from then one could speak in terms of a "new Basque diaspora,"[66] was the creation, under the 1978 Spanish Constitution, of the Basque Autonomous Government. This was a new form of local political administration with important levels of autonomy, and it gradually acquired more and more authority as regarded powers over Basque collectivities abroad. From then on and up to this day, there has been a strong effort within the administrative framework of the Basque Autonomous Government (composed mainly of the PNV) to maintain a sense of Basqueness outside the homeland. It designed different strategies and policies to implement and maintain this policy.

WILLIAM A. Douglass systematically outlines this development. Perhaps one of the most significant strategies regarding the Basque diaspora was the creation in 1982 of the Service for Relations with the Basque Centers. Then the first issue of the magazine *Euskal Etxeak* (literally meaning "Basque houses," but used as a means of describing the Basque centers) appeared in 1989. Existing to this day, the magazine aims at bringing the Basque Country and diaspora Basques closer together. Of no less importance was the creation of an annual budget that, since 1989, has been periodically increased, designed to cover certain financial expenses of the Basque centers and to provide educational material for teaching the Basque language and general cultural diffusion. Douglass also mentions the organization of the Conferences of Basque Collectivities, the granting of subsidies to help access the Internet from the centers in question, and the diffusion by satellite television of Euskal Telebista, the Basque TV station (see Section 2, Chapter 8). Other policies include the promotion of cultural encounters within each country, such as Basque cultural weeks.

THE MOST eloquent expression among all these measures, however, was perhaps the Basque Parliament's debate and later passage of the Law of Relations with the Basque Collectivities and Centers Abroad in 1994. Among other things, this established, at the request of the Basque Autonomous Government, an official Registry of Basque Centers, with a basic condition that the centers must be democratically constituted.

Viewed from the Basque Country, these measures both provoked disagreement with some Spanish parties (the PSOE and PP) and implied the creation of new networks of political negotiation for the Basque Autonomous Government, an outcome that was reinforced in 1993 with the creation of the Basque-Argentine Cooperation and Development Institute and similar institutions in Chile, Venezuela, and Mexico. All these institutes have specifically assigned roles that differ from those of the Basque centers. These organizations were trying to manage the flow of capital investment between the Basque Country and Latin America at a historic moment when the economies of the region in question began to open up to foreign investment. Yet these were all, in turn, initiatives that came to be seriously questioned by the central authority of the Spanish government. Specifically, it alleged that foreign management and representation

Collective Sentiment

Peer groups have been favorite sites of inquiry for social scientists interested in discovering the sociological distinctiveness of a particular place. Peer groups in contemporary Basque society are plural and heterogeneous, expressed in vastly different ways depending on variables such as a rural or urban environment, age and ethnolinguistic identity.

Illustration from Grandville's Un Autre Monde.

were not covered by the powers assigned to an autonomous government.

DIASPORA AND ETHNICITY

Independently of domestic political negotiations in the Basque Country, all these measures contributed and still contribute to reinforcing ethnic ties among Basques, whatever their place of residence. However, as Douglass also points out, the attributes of this Basqueness have been "defined from and by [the Basque Country] rather than in more parochial 'Argentine-Basque' or 'Australian-Basque' terms." Furthermore, he contends, "at times it is consciously pedagogical in that it seeks to educate hyphenated Basques (and interested non-Basques) regarding modern Old-World Basque reality, rather than reinforcing the fragmentary and stale stereotypes of it as transported abroad in the minds of emigrants leaving Europe one or more generations ago."[67] One should also point out that this process of ethnic reproduction is directed only at Spanish Basques, rather than at French Basque or Navarrese centers, even though the Basque Nationalist Party in government recognizes these regions as a part of the Basque Country.

IN GENERAL, these are strategies of ethnic reproduction that, from the Basque Country, and especially its governmental institutions, pursue the goal of internationalizing the legitimacy of ethnic nationalism.[68] However, the question of ethnicity is also one of power, because it creates both a center and a periphery. In this way, the process of ethnic promotion embarked upon several years ago has led to the issue becoming problematic, as evinced by the framing of different applications of negotiation and exchange that make up the agreement, not all of which have been undertaken without a measure of conflict regarding a response to the questions "Who are we," "What do we want," and "What will we be?"[69]

The response to these questions has provoked all kinds of debate between foreign Basques, often challenging the unilateral sense of ethnic definitions to the point of casting doubt on the denomination of the diaspora itself as such. And this led, above all, to a situation whereby certain Basque centers (such as several in Argentina), perhaps because they were made up in many cases of people from the economic and political elite of the country, were reticent about defining themselves as part of a diaspora.

THIS IS NOT only a matter of questioning and responding on the part of Basques abroad, but also something emerging as a form of public debate within the Basque Country itself. Indeed, the topic challenges the criteria of territoriality, and there are many who, underscoring the most optimistic facets of this process, are beginning to see a solution to the controversial and sometimes violent conflict of identities in the Basque Country. For the possibility of transcending territory to be recognized as Basque would imply eliminating the essence of the logical correlation in the conflict between Basque nationalism and the Spanish and French states as regards the attempt to achieve political control of this geographical space. Specifically, it would herald the possibility of feeling Basque beyond the originally inhabited territory, thereby overcoming not only distances between Basques in the Basque Country and those in the diaspora, but even between Basques in Spain and those living in Navarre and the French Basque Country.

Lesson eighteen

LEARNING OBJECTIVES

1. To be able to define diaspora as an emerging social phenomenon.
2. To be able to relate the concept of diaspora to that of ethnicity and identity.
3. To locate the principal historical developments contributing to making up the Basque diaspora.
4. To identify the dynamic between center and periphery (diaspora and place of origin) in reproducing ethnicity among Basques.

REQUIRED READING

William A. Douglass, "Creating the New Basque Diaspora," in *Basque Politics and Nationalism on the Eve of the Millennium*, ed. William A. Douglass, Carmelo Urza, Linda White, and Joseba Zulaika (Reno: Basque Studies Program, 1999), 208–28.

Gloria Totoricagüena, "Basques Around the World: Generic Immigrants or Diaspora?" *Euskonews & Media* 72 (March 2000), www.euskonews.com.

SUGGESTED READING

Kim Butler, "Defining Diaspora, Redefining a Discourse," *Diaspora* 10, no. 2 (2001): 189–219.

James Clifford, "Diasporas," *Cultural Anthropology* 9, no. 3 (1994): 302–38.

WRITTEN LESSON FOR SUBMISSION

1. Describe the dilemmas surrounding the globalization process as regards the dynamic between the local and the global and situate the diaspora phenomenon within such dilemmas.

2. Describe the potential of the diaspora phenomenon as regards the production/reproduction of ethnic attributes in the Basque case.

Gabriel Gatti (with the collaboration of Andrés G. Seguel)

19 · New forms of identity

SUMMARY

Throughout Section 3, we have addressed changes affecting social representations in politics (Chapter 13), language (Chapter 14), different generations (Chapter 15), work (Chapter 16), gender (Chapter 17), and territory (Chapter 18). Now we will attempt to take stock of all these transformations, asking what is happening today and how we might explain the contemporary shape of collective identity in the Basque Country. Our conclusion is that, faced with the univocal, unambiguous, and circular nature of identity in previous eras, the current social panorama points toward a multiplication of identities, a growing flexibility, and even the possibility of thinking about partial, ephemeral identities as the dominant forms today. We will close this chapter on new forms of identity with an analysis of one specific case: the San Francisco neighborhood in Bilbao.

FROM WHAT has been written so far, the reader will have been able to deduce the basic phenomena associated with, and the force of, social change in Basque society today: new social actors and agents, different socialization processes, new and varied ways of understanding politics, gender, work, and so on. These have been changes directly affecting identity. In this final chapter about society in the Basque Country, we will try to offer some sociological approaches that help us to understand contemporary Basque society by focusing on a topic we have underscored more than once: identity. This is because identity has always formed the main focus of attention for Basque sociology. It still is, but now the main focus is on the way it is changing.

COLLECTIVE IDENTITY: CONCEPTS AND CRISIS

Speaking about collective identity implies thinking about how a group of social actors construct a shared, stable, and lasting consciousness of belonging to a collective. Or at least this has been the case up until now. We are dealing with one of the most elusive concepts in social science. Up to now, the idea of a collective identity has served to think about how essential, homogeneous, and identity-based notions have been unambiguously maintained. However, now we are witnessing precisely the opposite features: variety, change, and instability—ideas that characterize contemporary identities.

THE PROBLEM is certainly not alien to the social sciences, which in their approach to the subject have tended to equate this term with two figures, the nation-state and the individual citizen, both seen as stable, homogeneous, and lasting, as well as political and institutional. This is not just a scarcely adequate imaginary for some social formations, but it is also, without any doubt, completely insufficient to comprehend contemporary societies. Indeed, this is so much the case that, today, such a model of identity is facing a crisis: Systems of classifying have been turned upside down, the lines between identities have been blurred, and social actors have been compromised by diverse loyalties, participating in different traditions. As a result of all this, more complex forms of identity and culture have emerged among contemporary social actors: hybrid, dual, multiple, and weak identities. These require ways of understanding identity as processed simultaneously by different cultures that relativize traditions, parody original models, and produce forms of membership that blend what before could not be mixed up, identity a constructed from a sort of day-to-day bricolage.[70] Naturally, the Basque Country has not been immune

New Basques
A store selling African goods in the San Francisco neighborhood of Bilbao, Bizkaia. An example of the increasingly visible nature of "everyday bricolage" in redefining contemporary identity in the Basque Autonomous Community. In San Francisco, many different cultures meet and mix.
Photo: Iñaki Martínez de Albeniz.

---

to these trends, and what follows is an overview of the changes associated with the idea of collective identity.

IDENTITY IN THE BASQUE COUNTRY

ADDRESSING only those sectors close to Basque nationalism, we have repeatedly argued in this book that Basqueness was imagined during the initial phase of Basque nationalism primarily on the basis of cultural-biological differentiation. This imaginary underwent its first transformation during the 1960s, when the community was conceived of as resistance, and "shared clandestinity"[71] was the predominant value. From then on, participation in a political community, not race, became the centerpiece of its activity. Basque identity was from that time on a political identity.

A whole dense network of communal spaces (explored in Section 2) supported this transformation: the family (Section 2, Chapter 5), *ikastolas* (Section 2, Chapter 7), the church (Section 2, Chapter 9), and the associative world (Section 2, Chapter 6)—locations capable of strengthening relationships and constructing identity, locations where individuals could experience and reproduce their collective history. These visible spaces in the community were truly anthropological places.[72] Above all, these were spaces reserved for members of the national community that they reproduced and were closed to those who did not possess the features that the community defined. The threshold that separated those who could and couldn't occupy these spaces of identity was previous membership, the force that united the agents with the features that made up and demonstrated the existing representation of identity.

THE PASSAGE of the Statute of Gernika solidified the Basque nationalist imaginary, although the administrative cohesion of nationalism was also accompanied by another process: the demobilization of the national community, the sustenance and basic condition for allowing the reproduction of a consciousness of belonging during the Franco era. The institutionalization of the nationalist imaginary allowed an administrative strengthening of the criteria associated with shaping a new sense of belonging, and this same mechanism led to an increasing social ambiguity.

This doesn't mean that the community or its base values disappeared, but rather that it lost its political content. The consolidation of the process of political institutionalization changed the general tendency of transformation processes in the Basque Country: As opposed to earlier eras, marked by a strong politicization of everyday life, what emerged was a new, less exceptional, and colder logic out of which identity became something more practical and less transcendent. With the institutionalization of the Basque nationalist imaginary, as well as the mechanisms by which it was reproduced and maintained, belonging was no longer a question of exclusive identities, but could also be understood in terms of partial identifications: sometimes one was Basque and on other occasions not. Sometimes being Basque meant one thing, and other times it meant something else. Identity was "softened" and made more flexible, malleable, and adaptable. Belonging thus became more open to the wider community.

A NEW GENERAL OVERVIEW OF IDENTITY IN THE BASQUE COUNTRY

A PROCESS began that allowed one to compare new readings of identity. Thus, cultural expressions characteristic of modern society have begun to take shape in the Basque Country, where, as one observer contends, ethnicity and cultural difference have lost their former importance, to be increasingly replaced by other forms of more flexible identity markers[73] Basque identity started to operate in the "supermarket of identity," negotiating the previously impermeable and now porous limits of the national community in order to become a container of multiple identifications, although this has hardly been a phenomenon unique to the Basque Country. Indeed, Basque identity went on

Neighborhood activism
An example of new identities and lifestyles. A flyer advertising a street market in the San Francisco neighborhood, Bilbao, including the possibility of directly exchanging goods without any monetary transaction. While the cultural makeup of San Francisco is nontraditional, its neighborhood activities resemble similar initiatives throughout Basque society.
Courtesy of Asociación de Comerciantes Dos de Mayo.

to integrate a series of highly volatile and tremendously flexible cultural expressions.

ONE MIGHT, then, for all the above reasons, argue that the following features have most effectively structured identity in the Basque Country following the process of political institutionalization. Identities in the Basque Country are going through a period of more and more uncertainty, with a growing blurring of intercommunal boundaries. Identities in the Basque Country also have reduced their political content and invested themselves with a more diffuse nature that is impossible to understand from the previous logic, that of the all-encompassing point of view of politics. Identity in the Basque Country is no longer constructed only in the realm of the national community, but also in the colder, less noteworthy spaces of institutionalization. The communities of reference for social identities are now nonexcluding, multiple, and open to combination.

Where and when is identity constructed in the Basque Country today? The public realm, a central reference point of social life in the Basque Country during the Franco era, has retreated, and in its place, an infinite number of microspaces of interaction have emerged. Indeed, this is the central hypothesis here: Beginning with the process of institutionalization, identity has been emptied of its political connotations and opened up to practices associated with everyday life, which in turn has encouraged the emergence of new areas of meaning.

If one considers the emergent forms of social life among young people (Section 2, Chapter 6; Section 3, Chapter 15), one sees the most striking change. New forms of youth social life are unfolding: on street corners, sidewalks, crossroads, and in other transitory spaces, spaces of youth sociality hardly unusual when compared with other everyday practices, but extremely different from the traditional experience of social life in the Basque Country.[74] Indeed, the political realm has given way to leisure and enjoyment through a growing transcendence of the inherent nature of the close and direct: Concert halls, nighttime places, and sites of mass consumption now form the terrain of these new identities, practical spaces for an emergent sociality that, to the extent that they do not allow one to get trapped in the political imaginary, disconcert those generations that experienced social life in the public realm and their identity in the political sphere.[75]

THESE ARE all specific spaces (since the reproduction of identity is not guaranteed) where identity adopts new forms, spaces shaped by an unprecedented inclusiveness in the recent history of the Basque Country, spaces, in sum, where one can detect movement or strategies involving the management and attribution of social meaning, that respond to emerging processes into whose functioning (once the importance of traditional logics have been discarded) one must enter in order to understand the future tendencies of society and identity in the Basque Country. Let's examine, then, by way of a conclusion, a paradigmatic case that synthesizes these new identity management strategies.

EMERGENT SOCIALITIES IN THE SAN FRANCISCO NEIGHBORHOOD

In Bilbao, until the 1960s, industrial activity principally defined dominant forms of both urbanization and social activity. However, as a result of economic decline in the 1980s and the concomitant downfall of this industrial activity, a series of structural transformations took place: a change in the labor market, rising unemployment, the growth of new methods of contracting labor, the development of an unofficial economy, a change in the occupational structure (owing to a growing number of technicians and declining number of industrial workers), and the spatial downsizing of the industrial structure through a number of closures.

The process of transformation currently taking place, which attempts to counteract this decline through policies of urban restructuring, has been termed the renewal of Bilbao. This effort has embraced a series of initiatives with a more or less common goal: to give a real impulse to the specialized tertiary economic sector, focusing on the revitalization of urban industrial spaces and the creation of new focuses of urban centrality.

Added to the influence of global trends, these structural transformations have had major repercussions in the local social life of Bilbao's neighborhoods. In fact, they have provoked innovative strategies on the part of those who live in the city and define their quality of life within its urban context, generating multiple social interpretations of the new in such a way that the whole phenomenon of change has allowed for the emergence of new spaces of sociality whose dynamic can be seen in the novel transformations of sectors and neighborhoods with formerly well-defined characteristics. This is the case of the San Francisco neighborhood in Bilbao.

THIS DISTRICT, socially removed from (yet geographically close to) the commercial and administrative center of Bilbao, has been transformed into a space embracing new lifestyles, nighttime entertainment, and, more recently, property speculation. Businesses here are mainly owned by immigrants and are situated in the same multiple-identity reference area. San Francisco as a place allows one to move from one space to another and to get to know people in numerous different ways in a reduced geographical space.

In this journey, new, nonformalized relations emerge, and personal relationships become permanent, diverse, and novel stimuli to a blurring of the boundaries imposed by the norms and rules of regular interaction, which at the same time remain powerful. What might seem, a priori, a problem—the thick and dense nature of activity here—actually generates a special attractiveness.

There is a dynamic interaction between the neighborhood's most typical (yet varied) situations and places: Here one can, for example, buy a loaf of bread in a bakery or café, find a small market open until the early hours of the morning, enter a Chinese store for some late-night shopping, visit a Pakistani delicatessen, and stop off to have a Berber tea on the way home, at the same time as seeing older men, the so-called *txikiteros*, wearing their *txapelas*, or berets, smoking cigars and undertaking the traditional *poteo*, going from bar to bar (see Section 2, Chapter 6), or visiting a more traditional grocery store located between Nigerian or Senegalese shops. This diversity, arranged in a historically well-known space, represents contemporary experiences unthinkable in other sociospatial contexts in Bilbao or even in the Basque Country in general.

THE SAN FRANCISCO neighborhood, insofar as it exemplifies the most classic forms of socialization together with new spaces of youth leisure, commerce, and the movement of immigrant groups, has encouraged a form of urban sociability that uses various spaces as mobile and changing places according to the activity in question, spaces defined according to the time of day and the groups inhabiting them at that moment, making up unfixed points of reference for urban journeys.

Here one sees another Bilbao, that of new ways of using space and new emerging social forms: bars facilitating conversation or providing specific forms of music and various kinds of DJs (gay, lesbian, techno, world, and Basque music, disco, or others). On certain days, this results in a coming together of young people from different areas and socioeconomic origins.

THIS DEMONSTRATES the existence of new emerging spaces that shelter places in permanent transformation, constructed and reconstructed through social activity. Through these forms, which recombine both old and new forms of identity and break down institutionalized meanings, there is a move toward forming new ways of constructing social sense based on multiple forms of relationship, all basic displacements in the emergence of these new social habits.

Lesson nineteen

LEARNING OBJECTIVES

1. To understand the problems involved today in framing a sociological notion of identity.
2. To understand the nature of socially constructed collective identity in the Basque Country during the Franco era.
3. To understand the influence that the political institutionalization of Basque nationalism has had on changing the logic of identity in the contemporary Basque Country.
4. To understand the nature of newly emerging social forms in the contemporary Basque Country.

REQUIRED READING

William A. Douglass, Carmelo Urza, Linda White, and Joseba Zulaika, eds., *Basque Politics and Nationalism on the Eve of the Millennium* (Reno: Basque Studies Program, 1999).

Joseba Zulaika, *Guggenheim Bilbao Museoa: Museums, Architecture, and City Renewal* (Reno: Center for Basque Studies, 2002).

SUGGESTED READING

Marc Augé, *Non-Places: Introduction to an Anthropology of Supermodernity* (London: Verso, 1995).
Celeste Olalquiaga, *Megalopolis: Contemporary Cultural Sensibilities* (Minneapolis: University of Minnesota Press, 1992).

WRITTEN LESSON FOR SUBMISSION

1. Critically assess the concept of identity and the changes that affect it in contemporary society.
2. Compare and contrast the changes that are occurring in the San Francisco neighborhood in Bilbao with another you know of in a sociocultural sphere closer to your own everyday experience.

Iñaki Martínez de Albeniz (with the collaboration of Gabriel Gatti and Ignacio Irazuzta)

Epilogue

Toward a sociology of Basque sociology

WE BEGAN this work with two questions: "What is the Basque Country? Or rather, what are we referring to when we talk about the Basque Country?" Such questions imply a referential premise. That is, they assume the existence of a social reality "out there somewhere" of which sociology should be careful to take note. However, even a basic overview of this topic reveals that Basque sociology, once institutionalized as the province of expert observers and as a transmitter of reflexive knowledge about society during the last thirty years (as, we believe, has been successfully demonstrated in this work), has also contributed to shaping this same society. Consequently, the time has come to confront this idea in the form of a hypothesis, a premise that might be termed the joint making of Basque society and Basque sociology. Thus, we might still pose the question about what Basque society is, but it would be difficult to sustain (as a referentialist would) that there could ever be a completely innocent answer to such a question, given that all such answers would potentially imply something about the questioner. Recognizing this point, as we will see, has major implications for the relationship between sociology and society. It is our task here to outline a general hypothesis about this joint construction of Basque society and Basque sociology and to profile the new approaches toward both, rather than develop them in extenso.

One of the consequences of the growing complexity and level of societal institutionalization is the fact that it has encouraged the emergence of a scientific subsystem from which society can observe itself. To think about society is to think sociologically. From this it follows that sociology not only observes and describes the social realm, but that, to a great extent, it also reflexively contributes to shaping it. However, it would not be very sociological to defend such a constructivist position without also reflexively mentioning the sociological conditions that make it feasible. Put another way, we must be aware of the fact that constructivist turn is not the effect of some assumed generational wisdom. Rather, it fits in with (or is tied to) the accumulation of specific theoretical, historical, and generational facts and conditions. Liberally adapting Marx's theory of (economic) surplus, one might say that only the academic surplus produced during the early foundational and institutional phase of Basque sociology made the idea of sociology examining itself and measuring its performative effects on reality plausible.

BASQUE anthropology served as an antecedent of this constructivist and reflexive turn in sociology when it turned in on itself. Indeed, the work of some anthropologists[76] has unreservedly demonstrated how, through the first half of the twentieth century, the practice of anthropological representation gave shape to the notion of Basqueness. It helped model an idea of origins, contributed to building a meaningful time frame, and contributed to establishing a historical continuity. As Joseba Zulaika argues, the scientific discourse of anthropology undertook a narrative and categorical closure of Basqueness and its model subject, and it did so with a powerful rhetoric, establishing an origin and cementing the myth of an autochthonous race by "assuming that biological evolution itself was autochthonous in the Basque case."[77] In this way, Basque anthropology achieved a number of things. It prescribed an *original moment* of Basqueness. It constructed a historical framework that linked this moment to the present. And it identified a

Selling culture
A souvenir store in Bilbao, Bizkaia. Another means and another use of culture: the marketing of Basque culture. For visitors to the (global) Guggenheim, there are plenty of opportunities for (local) purchases.
Photo: Iñaki Martínez de Albeniz.

---

subject associated with this origin, identifying the social places where the subject survived: a space (the rural environment), together with certain cultural features and practices (a non-Romanized subject, linguistically and biologically autochthonous, and so on). Thanks to this work, the specificity and authenticity of Basqueness became cultural and scientific totems.

ONE CAN detect a certain familial bond between what anthropology did before and what sociology is now capable of doing. Basque anthropology undertook this labor first because it had sufficiently outlined an object of analysis from which it could distance itself in the interests of reflexively observing it.[78] Now, however, as the object of Basque sociology—Basque society—has achieved a level of (evident and plausible) institutionalization, and sociology (in good part thanks to the work of sociology itself) has achieved a sufficient level of disciplinary maturity, it is ready to take the same route.

BASQUE SOCIOLOGY AS AN OBJECT OF STUDY

In this epilogue, we can hope only to outline briefly the main points of what we term a sociology of Basque sociology. The central idea here, we repeat, is the joint making of both society and sociology, a joint making in the sense that the relationship between society and sociology has had a dual direction.

On the one hand, sociology shapes (or contributes to the shaping of) the social realm, and (Basque) society doesn't constitute a given, permanent reality. Rather, it is in good part shaped by what sociology says about (or how it represents) it. As a result, Basque society is an object that is subject to various controversies or different ways in which Basque sociology has come to represent it.

ON THE OTHER hand, society *reacts* (although not in an intentional way) to these representations or, to a certain extent, *objects* to them. To argue that only sociology and sociologists achieve reflexive understanding is to ignore the fact that in today's complex, so-called information societies, the distinction between science and ethnoscience is more and more diffuse. That is why, the "objections" of society to what sociology says about and does with it (through the representations it elaborates) should not be understood as a deliberate, conscious reaction. If sociology makes scientific knowledge social, once this knowledge is returned to society, that is, once it is socialized—and becomes ethnoscientific—it activates social change and leads to still further social complexity, here in the form of unwanted consequences that once again sociology must face from a scientific point of view.

It is not, then, a question of limiting the inquiry into *what* Basque society is. As a consequence of the constructivist turn, the questions to which we alluded at the beginning of the epilogue have to be reformulated: Is Basque society the same after the institutionalization of Basque sociology? How does one contribute to the shaping of the other? The answer to these questions inevitably involves considering Basque sociology itself as an object of study: to undertake a history and sociology of Basque sociology. Only from this starting point can we begin to speak about the tense and complex relationship between Basque sociology and the social realm, since in good part its history is the story of these tensions.

IN GOOD measure, if it's a matter of addressing these new questions, the pretext and meaning of a work about Basque society reveal other issues. What might have been, until now, a more or less careful and accurate description of Basque society would thus become a more condensed version or sampling of the distinct sociological perspectives delimiting its perimeters. Thus, the tensions and controversies between these perspectives—that mutually need and explain one another, and that in so doing make up a conceptual network—would *controversially* shape the object that is "Basque society." Put another way, they would make this subject a contentious one.

The criteria for delimiting a sociology of Basque sociology are potentially numerous, but for a systematic picture of the different perspectives struggling to represent Basque society, we would highlight two that seem especially relevant. The first is theoretical or a synchronic and esoteric criterion, since it is scarcely affected by

Investing in technology
Since 1985, the Zamudio Technology Park in Bizkaia has been a center for companies focused on new technologies. A public initiative, the park is a flagship project encouraging research and development.
Photo: Iñaki Martínez de Albeniz.

---

historical contingency or factors external to sociological discourse itself. The second is historical (and by extension generational).As opposed to the previous criterion, it possesses a diachronic and exoteric nature, being composed of historical time and the social context in which different sociological perspectives appeared.

AN OUTLINE OF THE CONCEPTUAL FRAMEWORK OF BASQUE SOCIOLOGY

It is clear, from the perspective of Basque sociology's various (meta)theoretical proposals, that the relationship between the theoretical references on which the three sections of this book are based should be reconsidered. Specifically, we should think critically about the objectivity/factual nature of the social or the *hard* part of society (Section 1), the subjectivization or *socialization* of this objective order, or the *soft* part of society (Section 2), and the crisis of articulating both demands (Section 3)—that is, on the one hand, about social institutions (politics, religion, work, and so on) and, on the other, forms of subjectivization and the social meanings they promote. From a constructivist perspective, these references (structure, meaning, subjectivity, identity, and so on) cease to be inherent characteristics (or features) of society and come to be considered as theoretical devices through which to observe (and shape) the social realm.

WE ARGUE, by way of a tentative hypothesis, that as regards its theoretical proposals, Basque sociology has shifted from oscillating between two flexible ways of looking at society in a synthesis between the material and normative aspects of society; that is, between the factual nature of structure (from the Durkheimian tradition) and the subjective sense of action (from the Weberian tradition), to a third, postclassical perspective that, as regards its theoretical foundation, starts from a questioning of the objectivist/subjectivist synthesis, tightens the limits of the discipline itself, and opens itself up to a certain theoretical and methodological eclecticism.

We will outline, without claiming to be exhaustive, but also avoiding falling into oversimplification, each of these perspectives. The first perspective's theoretical devices, centering on a factual view of society, address the objectivity and permanence of society. It has a theoretical preference for structure (the transverse or leveling concept of reality par excellence), and it attempts methodologically to describe (more than to understand) the different structural fields or realms that make up a fully instituted society with clear profiles (to a certain extent reflecting historical change): politics, language, the economy, population, culture, and so forth.

THE THEORETICAL devices used by the second perspective emphasize not so much the factual nature or stability of a society's structure, but the subjective meaning of action, the *meaning* of the social realm. While the first perspective suspends the social realm within the structure, this second perspective is affected by the inertia of development from traditional to modern societies. The question of social meaning is therefore equivalent to that of the meaning of modernity: the "teleology" of modernization processes, the bases of social reproduction, and the shaping centers of the social realm and meaning.

The basic difference of the third perspective, here termed "postclassical" (although it would not be inappropriate to call it "postmodern"), in regard to the second one is that, far from asking questions about the meaning that underpins modern society, it openly declares a crisis in society and witnesses the spectacle of efforts to confront the crisis on the part of social actors that deploy new subjectivities (identities). This represents a sociological perspective embracing a new empiricism in a more "emphatic" way than the first one. Clearly, then, these three perspectives are not mutually exclusive. In fact, as mentioned above, they need and question one another and together make up the whole conceptual framework that we call Basque sociology.

THE HISTORICAL, SOCIAL, AND GENERATIONAL CONTEXT OF BASQUE SOCIOLOGY

If a sociology of (Basque) sociology relied only theoretical criteria that are esoteric or internal to the discipline, it would be difficult to understand for people removed from academic debate. The second of the above criteria concerning a potential sociology of Basque sociology, the historical/generational perspective, remedies this. This criterion is the product of the combined activity of two forces: the historical context in which the different sociological perspectives arose and what Karl Mannheim has termed the "generational entelechy,"[79] that is, the experience of specific historical events on the part of generations that embody them.

Broadly speaking, we would argue that the first of the above-mentioned perspectives is fully inscribed in the rhetoric and practice of institutions to the extent being one of their principal allies. Its vocation is to serve as a storehouse of knowledge and a legitimizing factor in order to make decisions in such matters as economic planning, resolving social problems, or cultural promotion. It is a perspective intimately linked to the administration and with a *statistical* calling in the literal sense of the term: It is, in other words, a science of state. Consequently, it is hardly coincidental that this perspective finds its true raison d'être in what we have termed the process of political institutionalization.

THE SECOND perspective has, without doubt, less of a liking for professionalization and social intervention. Its vocation is, rather, academic, and the scholarly realm also marks the limits of its articulation. Here, historicist sensitivity to social processes, absent in the previous perspective, particularly stands out. This is hardly surprising, because the generation of sociologists that personified this perspective were for the most part socialized during the Franco era. Out of this traumatic experience came a preoccupation with the transition from tradition to modernity and the need to construct a sociological narrative about modernization processes.

Finally, the third perspective is located in a historical moment when the social and sociological models that the second perspective attempted to consolidate are entering a period of crisis. It is composed of greater theoretical and methodological eclecticism and reveals a certain tendency toward interdisciplinary approaches. Against it, there is a certain lack of attention to historicity. This is perhaps the result of a stability caused by political institutionalization, a context that, one should not forget, has implied both Basque sociology's very condition of existence and sphere of articulation, while at the same time reducing the intense nature of historical experience and generational reflexivity. It is, however, a perspective in constant dialogue with the second one, and this dialogue allows it to share with its counterpart an academic vocation. It is, in sum, both a vicarious perspective, since it is constructed against the previous example, and a parasitic perspective, since it uses its surplus to (among other things) undertake a sociology of sociology.

Glossary

Ajuria-Enea Pact: An agreement aimed at achieving the normalization of, and an end to violence in, the Basque Country, signed on January 12, 1988 by all Basque political parties with the exception of the radical Basque nationalist Herri Batasuna.

Alarde: A military-style parade, held annually in the Gipuzkoan border towns of Irún and Hondarribia, commemorating the existence of municipal militias that fought against French occupation. At present, these celebrations have turned into a contentious issue regarding the demands of women to take part in them alongside men as part of the militias, a traditionally male role, and thereby to renounce the traditional female role of *cantinera*, or serving girl.

Basque Autonomous Community (BAC): An autonomous community in the Spanish state, according to the 1979 Statute of Gernika, composed of the historic territories of Araba, Gipuzkoa and Bizkaia.

Batzoki: A bar-restaurant open to the general public where members and sympathizers of the Basque Nationalist Party generally meet.

Carlism: A conservative political ideology created in the nineteenth century to defend traditional society against the rising force of liberalism.

Concierto Económico: See Fiscal Pact.

Cuadrilla: Large peer groups or groups of friends.

Diputación/Diputaciones: See Provincial Council.

Emakunde: The Basque Women's Institute.

Erdaldun: In Euskara, literally a "possessor of a foreign language" or someone who neither understands nor speaks Basque. By extension, this has come to mean a speaker of Spanish or French in the southern and northern Basque Country respectively.

ETA: Euskadi 'ta Askatasuna, Basque Homeland and Liberty. Founded in 1959, an organization dedicated to using an armed struggle in pursuit of Basque independence.

Euskal etxeak: In Euskara, literally "Basque houses," or Basque centers, outside the Basque Country. They are generally cultural-recreational centers, although in recent years there have been calls to give them a greater say in questions related to the political representation of the Basque Country in other countries.

Euskaldun: In Euskara, literally "a possessor of Euskara," or someone who understands and speaks Basque, whether literate in the language or not.

Euskaldunberri or Neo-Basque speaker: In Euskara, literally "a new possessor of Euskara," or someone whose mother tongue is not Basque and who understands and speaks it well.

Euskaltegi: An educational center for teaching Euskara to adults.

Euskaltzaindia: The Academy of the Basque Language.

Euskal Telebista (ETB): The Basque public television service.

Euskara: The Basque language, also written Euskara.

Fiscal Pact: A law establishing the right of the Basque Autonomous Community to establish, maintain, and regulate the tax system within its region.

Foral: An adjective expressing being of or pertaining to the *fueros*.

Foral Community of Navarre: An autonomous community in the Spanish state, according to the 1982 Law of Foral Improvement in Navarre, composed of the province of Navarre.

Franco: General Francisco Franco, 1892–1975. Leader of the Spanish Nationalist forces that overthrew the Second Republic (1931–36) in the Spanish Civil War (1936–39) and later head of both the Spanish government (until 1973) and state (until 1975, the year of his death).

Fueros: From medieval times, each of the Basque provinces had special charters, known as *fueros*, that determined the nature of their administrative relationship with Castile (and later Spain) and defined the rights of their citizenry. These charters allowed the Basque provinces a degree of autonomy in their dealings with Spain and encouraged a strong local political tradition. After a series of civil wars in nineteenth-century Spain and an administrative reorganization of the country, the last *fueros* (with the exception of the Fiscal Pact) were abolished in 1876.

Gaztetxe: In Euskara, literally a "young people's house." Unofficial social centers generally organized and run by young people.

Greater Bilbao: An expression used to designate the city of Bilbao and its wider metropolitan area, the principal urban center of the Basque Country.

Hegoalde: In Euskara, literally "the southern side," or the South Basque Country, situated in the Spanish state. It is composed of the historic territories of Araba, Gipuzkoa, and Bizkaia (the Basque Autonomous Community) and Navarre (the Foral Community of Navarre).

Historic territory: Provinces that make up an intermediate administrative level between the Basque Autonomous Government and the local municipalities (city halls), whose government organs, the provincial councils, possess important political and especially fiscal powers.

Iparralde: In Euskara, literally "the northern side," or the North Basque Country, situated in the French state. It is composed of the provinces of Lapurdi, Zuberoa, and Benafarroa.

Ikastola: Grade and high schools that use Euskara as the language of instruction.

Law of Historic Territories: Known by its acronym in Spanish, LTH (Ley de Territorios Históricos), it aimed to establish a decentralized system and delegate power to the provincial councils (diputaciones).

Lehendakari: The president of the Basque Autonomous Community.

Partial Neo-Basque Speakers: Someone whose mother tongue is not Euskara and who speaks Basque with some difficulty or who, although not speaking it, does understand or read it well.

Poteo: The collective ritual of going from bar to bar, having small glasses of wine or beer, typically undertaken by *cuadrillas*.

Provincial council: An organ of government in each of the historic territories that possesses important fiscal powers.

Quasi-Euskaldun: Someone who either understands Euskara well or with some difficulty and who speaks it with some difficulty or not at all.

Spanish Civil War: The consequence of a military revolt against the elected government of Spain in 1936 that broke out into full-scale civil war and lasted until 1939.

Statute of Gernika: A Constitutional Law emanating from the 1978 Spanish Constitution and passed by referendum in 1979 by which the Basque Country acquired institutional status as an autonomous community within the Spanish state.

Contributors

Igor Ahedo, PhD in political science. Researcher at the Universidad Complutense, Madrid (Chapter 11).

Beatriz Cavia, BSc in sociology. Researcher at the Center for Studies on Collective Identity (Chapter 17).

Gabriel Gatti, PhD in sociology. Associate professor of sociology at the University of the Basque Country. Coordinator of the Center for Studies on Collective Identity (editor; Introduction, Chapters 7, 14, and 19).

Ignacio Irazuzta, PhD in sociology. Associate professor of sociology at the ITESM (Monterrey, Mexico). Researcher at the Center for Studies on Collective Identity (editor; Introduction, Chapters 5, 15, and 18).

Marta Luxan, PhD in geography. Associate professor of sociology at the University of the Basque Country (Chapter 3).

Idoia Martín, BSc in sociology. Associate professor of sociology at the University of the Basque Country (Chapter 1).

Iñaki Martínez de Albeniz, PhD in sociology. Associate professor of sociology at the University of the Basque Country. Researcher at the Center for Studies on Collective Identity (editor; Introduction, Chapters 2, 8, 13, and Epilogue).

Zesar Martínez, PhD in sociology. Associate professor of sociology at the University of the Basque Country (Chapter 6).

Alfonso Pérez-Agote, PhD in sociology. Professor of sociology at the Universidad Complutense, Madrid. President of the Center for Studies on Collective Identity (Chapter 9).

Elsa.Santamaría, BSc in sociology. Researcher at the Center for Studies on Collective Identity (Chapter 16).

Andrés G. Seguel, BSc in anthropology. Researcher at the Center for Studies on Collective Identity (Chapter 1, Chapter 19).

Benjamín Tejerina, PhD in sociology. Professor of sociology at the University of the Basque Country. Director of the Center for Studies on Collective Identity (Chapters 4, 10, and 12).

Notes

1. Before this date, the demographic statistics used here come from the *Instituto Nacional de Estadística* (National Statistics Institute) in Madrid.
2. See Anthony Giddens, *The Transformation of Intimacy: Sexuality, Love and Eroticism in Modern Societies* (Stanford: Stanford University Press, 1992).
3. See Jürgen Habermas, *The Structural Transformation of the Public Sphere: An Inquiry into a Category of Bourgeois Society* (Cambridge, Mass.: MIT Press, 1989).
4. David Sven Reher, "Familia y sociedad. El legado de la historia en el mundo contemporáneo," *Vasconia* 28 (1999): 11–27.
5. Ibid.
6. Manuel González Portilla and José Urrutikoetxea, "Familia vasca e historia: Entre el cambio y las resistencias," *Cuadernos del Alzate* 20 (1999): 205–18.
7. See José María Tápiz, "Ámbito familiar y transmisión ideológica. El caso del PNV durante la II República," *Vasconia* 28 (1999): 261–70.
8. CEIC (Centro de Estudios sobre la Identidad Colectiva), *Institucionalización política y reecantamiento de la socialidad: Las transformaciones del mundo nacionalista, Soziologiako euskal koadernoak / Cuadernos sociológicos vascos, no. 2* (Vitoria: Gobierno Vasco, 1999).
9. Ibid.
10. See Giddens, *The Transformation of Intimacy.*
11. Jesús Arpal, "Solidaridades elementales y organizaciones colectivas en el País Vasco (cuadrillas, txokos, asociaciones)," in *Processus sociaux, idéologies et pratiques culturelles dans la société basque*, ed.

Pierre Bidart (Pau: Université de Pau et des Pays de l'Adour; CNRS, 1985), 136.

12. "The *cuadrilla* does not sustain any deeper relations than intimacy. Members of the *cuadrilla* might find someone to confide their more personal or intimate problems in either among the *cuadrilla* itself, but [also] specific or concrete individuals, or even outside it." Alfonso Pérez-Agote, *El nacionalismo vasco a la salida del franquismo* (Madrid: CIS, 1987), 98.
13. Ibid., 138.
14. Ibid., 153.
15. Pierre Bourdieu, et al., *Reproduction in Education, Society and Culture* (London: Sage, 1990), Paul Willis, *Learning to Labour: How Working Class Kids Get Working Class Jobs* (Farnborough: Saxon House, 1977).
16. In line with the focus of this book, here I will exclusively address the particularities of the Basque primary and secondary education system, rather than exploring the university structure.
17. Taken from Pauli Dávila, "El modelo histórico de alfabetización en Euskal Herria," in *Lengua, escuela y cultura: El proceso de alfabetización en Euskal Herria, siglos XIX y XX*, ed. Pauli Dávila (Lejona: Servicio Editorial de la Universidad del País Vasco, 1995), 17–44.
18. And also, it should be said, of quite a few sociological preoccupations, since in the light of the emergency of the social problem of education, the first tentative sociological analyses began to emerge in the Basque Country.
19. Jesús Arpal, et al., *Educación y sociedad en el País Vasco* (Donostia: Txertoa, 1982), 45, 44, 51.
20. Ibid., 49.

21. CEIC, "Institucionalización política y reencantamiento de la socialidad: Las transformaciones del mundo nacionalista," *Soziologiazko euskal koadernoak / Cuadernos sociológicos vascos*, no. 2 (Vitoria: Gobierno Vasco, 1999).
22. CEIC (1999); Eugenia Ramírez Goicoechea, *De jóvenes y sus identidades: Socioantropología de la etnicidad en Euskadi* (Madrid: CIS-Siglo XXI, 1990).
23. Ramón Zallo, ed., *Industrias y políticas culturales en España y País Vasco* (Bilbao: Servicio Editorial de la Universidad del País Vasco, 1995), 199.
24. OJD, 1998. OJD is a trading company whose goal is to facilitate information about the circulation and distribution of newspaper publications.
25. Mikel Arriaga, Andrés Davila, and J. L. Pérez Soengas, "Difusión de los diarios en Euskalherria desde la transición política: De lo ordinal a lo cardinal," *ZER* 10 (2001), www.ehu.es/zer/zer10/arriaga.html.
26. Zallo, *Industrias y políticas culturales en España y País Vasco*, 214.
27. Luis Michelena, "El largo y difícil camino del euskara," in *El libro blanco del Euskara*, ed. Luis Michelena et al. (Bilbao: Euskaltzaindia, 1977), 19–20.
28 .Ibon Sarasola, *Historia social de la literatura vasca* (Madrid: Akal, 1976), 70
29. The role played by the Catholic Church in the Basque Country was similar to what Hank Johnston has observed regarding the case of Catalonia: "The central role played by the Catholic Church in Catalonia derives from two sources. Culturally, there is a historical linkage with a traditional form of nationalism. Structurally, special privileges accorded the church by the Franco regime made it one of the few places one could escape state scrutiny." See Hank Johnston, *Tales of Nationalism: Catalonia, 1939–1979*

(New Brunswick, NJ: Rutgers University Press, 1991), 50–51. Yet in the Basque case, the relationship between the (Basque) language and the church was essentially stronger, given the markedly rural nature of Basque during the Franco years and the social power and influence that the church had in the rural environment. On this subject, see Xabier Itcaina, "Catholicisme et identités basques en France et en Espagne: La construction religieuse de la référence et de la compétence identitaires," PhD diss., Institut d'Etudes Politiques, Université de Bordeaux IV, 2000, where he analyzes the historical role played by the clergy as regards the Basque language and culture and where he also explores the role played by seminaries and novitiates in constructing an identity-based competence, in the sense that Anthony Giddens means it in his *The Constitution of Society: Outline of the Theory of Structuration* (Cambridge: Polity Press, 1984), that is, of a competence in questions directly related to the construction and maintenance of Basque identity. This brought with it, to a certain extent, an intellectual role on the part of the clergy, given the absence of a relevant professional academic sector. In this sense, the establishment and development of a Basque public university has had very important secularizing consequences for the Basque intellectual environment during the post-Franco era (after 1975).

30. For a detailed account of this process see Joan Mari Torrealday, *Euskal idazleak gaur* (Oñate: Jakin, 1977), 356–58.
31. Sarasola, *Historia social de la literatura vasca*, 21. A similarly high number of seminarians later entered the radical Basque nationalist political world.

32. Although space limitations preclude a more detailed examination, one should mention here a significant change that took place in certain sectors of the church hierarchy as a result of the Vatican Council toward the end of the Franco regime. This resulted in an increasingly liberal discourse in the social and political field that had important consequences for the Basque church hierarchy's opinion about the Basque national question.
33. In order to do this, I have examined what today is the Basque Autonomous Community and Navarre, because the principal direct sources cover both areas and because the most religious part of Navarre is to be found in the north, where there is a strong Basque cultural presence. See Alfonso Pérez-Agote, *Los lugares sociales de la religión: La secularización de la vida en el País Vasco* (Madrid: Centro de Investigaciones Sociológicas, 1990). See also Itcaina, "Catholicisme et identités basques," where he analyzes the appearance of religion and, mainly, the clergy in nonreligious spheres of society, such as culture and language, the economy (through the cooperative movement), and political identity.
34. Luis C. Núñez, *Opresión y defensa en Euskera* (San Sebastián: Txertoa, 1977), 57.
35. Regarding the source cited there instead, in the *Anuario de la iglesia en España* (Madrid: Arias Montano, 1990), there are no figures for priests' ordinations.
36. Rogelio Duocastella et al., *Análisis sociológico del catolicismo español* (Barcelona: Nova Terra, 1967), 46.
37. Ibid., 46.
38. See Gurutz Jáuregui, *Ideología y estructura política de ETA* (Madrid: Siglo XXI, 1981).

39. See Guy Rocher, *A General Introduction to Sociology: A Theoretical Perspective* (New York: St. Martin's Press, 1972).
40. Giovanni Sartori, *Parties and Party Systems: A Framework for Analysis* (Cambridge: Cambridge University Press, 1976).
41. Following the arguments of Stein Rokkan, *Citizens, Elections, Parties* (Oslo: Universitetsforlaget, 1970) and Daniel-Louis Seiler, *Partis et familes politiques* (Paris: Presses Universitaires de France, 1980), this "center/periphery" cleavage pits families of centralist parties against those of regionalist, autonomist, federalist, or pro-independence ones.
42. Francisco Letamendia, *Game of Mirrors: Centre-Periphery National Conflicts* (London: Ashgate, 2000).
43. In the early 1990s, several leading figures in the PSOE government's Ministry of the Interior were jailed for either corruption or participating in a dirty war against ETA. Eventually, a general decline combined with a reduced legitimacy as a result of these events lead to the PSOE losing power at the state level, to be replaced by the PP under the leadership of José María Aznar in 1996.
44. Claus Offe, "Challenging the Boundaries of Institutional Politics: Social Movements Since the 1960s," in *Changing Boundaries of the Political: Essays on the Evolving Balance between the State and Society, Public and Private in Europe*, ed. Charles Maier (Cambridge: Cambridge University Press, 1987), 65.
45. Alberto Melucci, *Nomads of the Present: Social Movements and Individual Needs in Contemporary Society* (Philadelphia: Temple University Press, 1989), 44, 79.
46. Jean L. Cohen and Andrew Arato, *Civil Society and Political Theory* (Cambridge, Mass.: MIT Press, 1994).

47. Offe, "Challenging the Boundaries of Institutional Politics," 72.
48. Dieter Rucht, "The Strategies and Action Repertoires of New Movements," in *Challenging the Political Order*, ed. Russell J. Dalton and Manfred Kuechler (London: Polity Press, 1990), 162.
49. Melucci, *Nomads of the Present*, 145–46.
50. Jacqueline Urla, "Cultural Politics in an Age of Statistics: Numbers, Nations and the Making of Basque Identity," *American Ethnologist* 20, no. 4 (1993): 818–43.
51. Ibid., 830.
52. Helena Wulff, "Introducing Youth Culture in its Own Right: The State of the Art and New Possibilities," in *Youth Cultures: A Cross-Cultural Perspective*, ed. Vered Amit-Talai and Helena Wulff (London: Routledge, 1995), 7.
53. Eugenia Ramírez Goicoechea, *De jóvenes y sus identidades: Socioantropología de la etnicidad en Euskadi* (Madrid: CIS, 1991), Sharryn Kasmir, "'More Basque than You': Class, Youth and Identity in an Industrial Basque Town," *Identities: Global Studies in Culture and Power* 9 (2002): 39–68.
54. Alfonso Pérez-Agote, "The Future of Basque Identity," in *Basque Politics and Nationalism on the Eve of the Millennium.*, ed. William A. Douglass, Carmelo Urza, Linda White, and Joseba Zulaika (Reno: Basque Studies Program, 1999), 54–67.
55. To obtain labor statistics for the Basque Country, one can consult various sources: The Encuesta de Población Activa (EPA, Survey of the Active Population) of the Instituto Nacional de Estadística (National Statistics Institute), Población en Relación a la Actividad (PRA, Population in Relation to Activity) of the Instituto Vasco de Estadística (Basque

Statistics Institute), the Censo de Mercado de Trabajo (Labor Market Census), the Instituto Nacional de Empleo (INEM, National Employment Institute), and Eurostat, among others.

56. Richard Sennett, *The Corrosion of Character: The Personal Consequences of Work in the New Capitalism* (New York: W.W. Norton, 1998).
57. Workers cooperatives have been very important in the Basque Country, in particular, the Mondragón Corporación Cooperativa (MCC, the Mondragon Cooperative Corporation).
58. INEM (National Employment Institute).
59. See, for example, Manuel Castells, *The Information Age: Economy, Society, and Culture*, vol. 1, *The Rise of the Network Society* (Cambridge, Mass.: Blackwell, 1997).
60. Kim Butler, "Defining Diaspora, Redefining a Discourse," *Diaspora* 10, no. 2 (2001): 189–219.
61. James Clifford, "Diasporas," *Cultural Anthropology* 9, no. 3 (1994): 302–38.
62. Butler, "Defining Diaspora."
63. William Safran, "Diasporas in Modern Societies: Myths of Homeland and Return," *Diaspora* 1, no. 1 (1991): 83–84, cited in Clifford, "Diasporas," 305.
64. Taking into account the social productiveness of the diaspora phenomenon and its growing treatment by social science, many people have highlighted the significance of the term "diaspora" (at least in English and other Indo-European languages) sharing a clear root, through the consonants—"spr"—with such suggestive words as "spore," "disperse," "spread," and "sperm." See Khachig Tôlôyan, "Rethinking *Diaspora(s)*: Stateless Power in the Transnational Moment," *Diaspora* 5, no. 1 (1996): 3–36.

65. In Argentina, for example, Basques even formed a kind of pressure group that lobbied the government of President Ortiz to create a pro-Basque immigration committee in 1940, a measure instantly opposed by the diplomatic representatives of the Franco dictatorship, who managed to get it disbanded by Perón's government in 1947. In turn, this event marked a milestone in creating a sense of diaspora belonging among Basques in Argentina.
66. William A. Douglass, "Creating the New Basque Diaspora," in *Basque Politics and Nationalism on the Eve of the Millennium*, ed. William A. Douglass, Carmelo Urza, Linda White, and Joseba Zulaika (Reno: Basque Studies Program, 1999), 208–28.
67. Ibid., 210.
68. See Douglass, "Creating the New Basque Diaspora," 208–28.
69. "Nora goaz?" (Where are we going?) was the motto of the last Conference of Basque Collectivities, held in Vitoria (the capital of the Basque Autonomous Community) in 1999.
70. See Marc Augé, *Non-Places: Introduction to an Anthropology of Supermodernity* (London: Verso, 1995).
71. Alfonso Pérez-Agote, *La reproducción del nacionalismo vasco* (Madrid: CIS, 1984), 114.
72. See Augé, *Non-Places*.
73. On this general subject, see Celeste Olalquiaga, *Megalópolis: Contemporary Cultural Sensibilities* (Minneapolis: University of Minnesota Press, 1992).
74. CEIC, *Institucionalización política y reecantamiento de la socialidad: Las transformaciones del mundo nacionalista, Soziologiako euskal koadernoak / Cuadernos sociológicos vascos, no. 2* (Vitoria: Gobierno Vasco, 1999).

75. This explains in great part the lack of studies in the Basque Country focusing on everyday life. In effect, neither sociology nor anthropology—which are, still today, mainly political sociology and cultural anthropology—have not yet examined this line of research. Some interesting approaches to new forms of identity can be found in Augé, *Non-Places* and Olalquiaga, *Megalopolis*. As regards the Basque case, see William A. Douglass, Carmelo Urza, Linda White, and Joseba Zulaika, eds., *Basque Politics and Nationalism on the Eve of the Millennium* (Reno: Basque Studies Program, 1999) and *Institutionalización política y reecantamiento de la socialidad*.
76. See Jesús Azkona, *Etnia y nacionalismo vasco: Una aproximación desde la antropología* (Barcelona: Anthropos, 1984), Joseba Zulaika, *Del Cromañon al carnaval: Los vascos como museo antropológico* (Donostia: Erein, 1996), and Jacqueline Urla, "Cultural Politics in an Age of Statistics: Numbers, Nations and the Making of Basque Identity," *American Ethnologist* 20, no. (4 (1993): 818–43.
77. Zulaika, *Del Cromañon al carnaval*, 112–13.
78. It is also true that anthropology's object is less subject to historical fluctuation or contingency.
79. Karl Mannheim, "The Problem of Generations," in *Karl Mannheim's Sociology of Knowledge*, trans. A. Simonds (Oxford: Clarendon Press, 1978), 276–322.

Pictures

Index

A

B

C

F

G

K

L

M

N

O

P

R

S

T

U

Y

Z

Colophon

This book was edited by Bud Bynack and indexed by Melanie Piper. It was laid out and produced by Gunnlaugur SE Briem, who also designed the typeface, BriemAnvil.

The Basque Studies textbook series

1. Basque Cinema: An Introduction
2. Basque Culture: Anthropological Perspectives
3. Basque Cyberculture: From Digital Euskadi to CyberEuskalherria
4. Basque Diaspora: Migration and Transnational Identity
5. Basque Economy: From Industrialization to Globalization
6. Basque Gender Studies
7. Basque Society: Structures, Institutions, and Contemporary Life
8. Basque Sociolinguistics: Language, Society, and Culture
9. Guggenheim Bilbao Museoa: Museums, Architecture, and City Renewal
10. Modern Basque History: Eighteenth Century to the Present
11. Waking the Hedgehog: The Literary Universe of Bernardo Atxaga

www.ingramcontent.com/pod-product-compliance
Lightning Source LLC
La Vergne TN
LVHW020531100826
845148LV00010B/1412
9781877802256